ACCESS TO THE HISTORIC ENVIRONMENT

Meeting the needs of disabled people

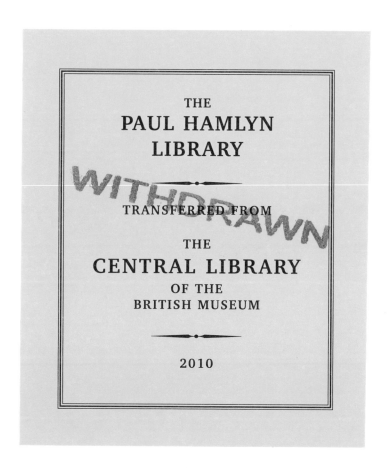

Dedication

For Andrew Walker. His courage and determination forces us to reconsider environmental design for old buildings and sites, and to find ways which protect the fabric and the dignity of the person.

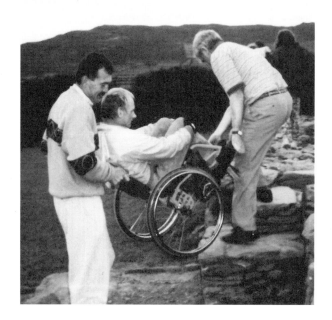

ACCESS TO THE HISTORIC ENVIRONMENT

Meeting the needs of disabled people

Lisa Foster

MA, Cons (York)

with
Foreword by Patrick Nuttgens CBE MA PhD ARIBA
and
Drawings by Charles Glen

DONHEAD

The right of Lisa Foster to be identified as the Author of the work has
been asserted by her in accordance with the Copyright, Designs and
Patents Act 1988

First published in the United Kingdom in 1997
Donhead Publishing
Lower Coombe
Donhead St Mary
Shaftesbury
Dorset SP7 9LY
Tel: (01747) 828422

ISBN 1 873394 18 7

A CIP catalogue record is available for this book from the British Library

Typeset and originated by Carnegie Publishing Ltd, Preston
Printed in Great Britain by The Bath Press, Bath

CONTENTS

FOREWORD

The title and subtitle of this book describe its purpose precisely – it is intended to 'meet the needs of disabled people'. And it does so in the most sensible – and accessible – manner. It lists exactly what any designer needs in terms of dimensions and spaces and slopes; and it gives case studies of the most varied types of historic building – everything from town halls to a converted prison.

Being myself an architect and architectural historian who has been seriously disabled, first by poliomyelitis and then by multiple sclerosis, I know at first hand how necessary the book is and how difficult it is to provide satisfactory access in historic environments. You might say – and I have often said – that the more valuable and historic a building is, the more difficult it will be to solve the problems of accessibility.

The challenge is greatest for the bodies that own the most beautiful historic buildings – like the churches and the National Trust. It seems to me ironic that, for example, people going to church never needed to go to the lavatory until today. And mothers and children have put up with almost impossible conditions in shops and schools and churches – even hospitals! And to make matters worse, there are organizations that will go to almost any length to prevent us from making changes in historic properties.

The fact is that any historic building must occasionally be modified and added to if it is to be a living and liveable asset. Conservation was defined as both preserving and enhancing the environment. Enhancement means change – and change is the very essence of history.

What change could be more valuable than making a historic environment accesible to all of us? If this book helps in that estimable aim, it will itself deserve a place among the changes of history.

Patrick Nuttgens CBE, MA, PhD, ARIBA

PREFACE

The value of many historic buildings and sites lies mainly in the evidence they display of change and development in our society. Alterations can reveal much about the community's response to shifting social, political and intellectual movements. An important conservation principle is acceptance of new layers and resistance to the removal of accretions. For the majority of historic buildings, there is no intrinsic conservation policy against adding layers to working buildings during our own epoch if done in a way that respects and preserves the existing cultural significance. Policy reasons suggest less intervention at cultural monuments than to working buildings. Appreciating this difference is an important factor in devising an access strategy for historic properties.

For a working building, adaptation may bring it up to contemporary safety, functional and social standards so ensuring its continued use and preservation. In this way, improved access will become part of the history of change, another layer of accretions to buildings to keep them in use. Importantly, whatever the level of provision, the changes will constitute evidence for future generations of the shift in attitude toward disabled people.

On a more pragmatic level, historic buildings make up a significant percentage of the existing built environment: they function as our places of work and accommodate our commercial and civic activities; they are our places of worship; and they provide us with places of leisure and cultural interest. As the disability movement has matured, so have the attitudes within the conservation community towards accepting physical change and loss of historic fabric in order to meet the needs of disabled people. Access alterations dedicated to wheelchair users which were too radical to consider a few years ago, have now been implemented (like the wheelchair platform lifts at Winchester Cathedral). These examples demonstrate a willingness by conservationists to meet the needs of disabled people in a manner consistent with the special architectural and historic interest of the building or site (see Figure P.1 below).

An important concept when devising an access strategy for historic properties is the recognition that by its nature, building conservation poses unique problems in each setting. Consequently, standard design guidance makes little sense. Each building or site presents its own particular opportunities and limitations. Integrated and independent access may be the ideal objective, but in practice different degrees of integration and independence may be achievable because of existing architectural features. The case studies in this book show the range of solutions possible.

This book is not intended to provide a detailed commentary on the access movement. The primary objective of my research was to collect and disseminate good practices as a source of reference and inspiration to others in resolving the dilemma of access to historic buildings and sites. Mindful of the reasons for taking a broad view of disability which includes people with sensory impairments and learning disabilities as well as old age, I nevertheless found that most alterations of buildings were done to achieve access for people who cannot negotiate steps. The explanations for this finding are obvious: the provision of level access for wheelchair users, for example, necessitates physical change to architectural features such as steps or it may require the installation of mechanical lift devices to overcome level changes. These types of changes require consent from conservation authorities, hence my focus on mobility-oriented solutions. There are many examples where access for

(a)

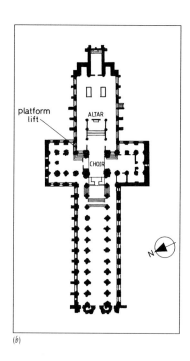

(b)

P.1 Winchester Cathedral.

(*a*) A wheelchair platform lift was installed in the North Transept to provide access to the raised retrochoir area. This location was considered to have the least impact on the historic fabric. The existing handrail was altered and a section hinged to allow the platform to pass. A neutral colour and discreet location, when in the closed position, minimizes the visual intrusion.

(*b*) Plan of the Cathedral shows location of platform lift at the steps in the North Transept.

wheelchair users was just one aspect of a comprehensive improvement in the facility. These examples illustrate the benefits of this shift in focus from *disabled access* to improved access for all and the recognition that disability prevalence rates increase significantly with age. Ageing itself makes it more difficult to move around, to see things and to hear things, even if the condition of being an *older* college tutor or parishioner is not considered disabled.

The other consistent theme of the case studies is that being carried is no longer considered an acceptable means of dignified access. This acceptance that dignity and the individual freedom from carrying is the minimum standard was developed in part from an article Selwyn Goldsmith wrote in 1983 on the so-called self-help movement in America. Whatever it had been in 1983, the thinking in the UK today has progressed so that integration and independence are accepted as the norm and freedom from carrying is the basis for dignified access. Not everyone has yet accepted this standard nor do all disabled people wish to exchange the element of personal care for an impersonal platform lift they cannot operate. This change in attitude and experience amongst both its advocates and disabled people will take time.

Case studies in this book are arranged according to the issue or issues being discussed, with varying levels of detail and information about the setting and the scheme. I felt that there would be too much repetition of detail if every building were treated as a separate study, since there is a consistent pattern of issues and solutions, despite the unique nature of each site.

Comprehensive technical guidance is beyond the scope of this book and readily available from other resources. I have developed a short assessment checklist for use in making an initial evaluation of existing features, as part of the process of devising an access strategy. Access design resources are included in the Bibliography, and the names of the firms of architects or local authorities involved in the work included in the Acknowledgements.

There is little discussion in the book on the provision of facilities for people with sensory impairments. A RNIB publication, *Building Sight* is recommended, and other references in the bibliography may be helpful, although there is an obvious need for further research and writing. This important area of work was beyond the scope of my initial research.

A shortcoming of the book which may be obvious to readers is that the author is able-bodied and that I have had to research and write from that perspective. The fact that I was not disabled did not even occur to me when I began research for this book in 1993 at the Institute of Advanced Architectural Studies in York. Then, as now, I was interested in countering the perception that good access provision for disabled people, primarily level access for wheelchair users, poses a threat to historic buildings and is irreconcilable with the conservation objectives.

As the research progressed, I realized that I myself was ignorant of the complex and dynamic issues surrounding the access debate. I knew about the Americans with Disabilities Act and was aware of the UK access movement to expand Part M of the Building Regulations to include alterations and to adopt comprehensive access legislation. An important question emerged in the literature about who the disabled are. Like so many others, I had equated the term 'access' with access for wheelchair users. Wheelchair users are not the only disabled people and access should not just be about ramps and handrails.

Changing the definition of who are disabled has affected the design approach in a fundamental way. Designing for wheelchair users alone can lead to separate routes and dedicated lift devices like the wheelchair platform lift, a device generally not usable by other disabled people. By refining the task to one of designing for accessibility, the emphasis has re-focused on solutions which provide level access in an integrated manner, meeting the needs of disabled people and others with limited mobility. This shift in design philosophy has occurred over the past few years while I was collecting the case study material.

One objective of the book is to inform those in conservation disciplines about access objectives and philosophy, in the same way that I came to the information – over time and piece by piece. This process helped me understand what the access objectives are and how they should influence design decisions. It is not just about the current legal requirements in the Disability Discrimination Act (which became law in the UK in November 1995) or complying with Building Regulations or the future EU directives. It has to do with the more ephemeral objectives of dignified, easy access; since how we care for people tells as much about our culture as the buildings and monuments we strive to protect.

L. F.
February 1997

ACKNOWLEDGEMENTS

Over the past four years the following people have generously given their time, assistance and encouragement in preparation of the manuscript. A special thanks is owed to Paul Velluet at English Heritage for reading the full text, and sharing his views in a most challenging historic venue, Gordon's Wine Bar, Central London.

John Adams, English Heritage

Nick Allen, Allen Todd Architects, Leeds

Sabrina Aaronovich, Access Committee of England

Sara Bairstow, Access Audit Consultants

John Barnes, English Heritage

David Brock, English Heritage

Lucinda Brown, Fan Museum, Greenwich

Dot Browning, plb architecture, formerly Plincke, Leaman & Browning

Phil Chambers, The Fieldfare Trust

Alison Coles, Museum & Galleries Commission

Gabrielle Coyle, Westminster City Planning

John Cumberland, Bolton Abbey

Jimmy Deenihan, TD, Co. Kerry, Ireland

John Edwards, English Heritage

Steve Farneth, Architectural Resources Group, San Francisco

Julie Fleck, Access Officer, Corporation of London

Anthony Foster

Martin Fox, Lawray Architects

Keith Garner, Architect, London

Ken Hampson, Architect, London

Judy Hawkins, English Heritage

Alan Hazelwood, Surveyor to Middle Temple

Frank Kelsall, English Heritage

Sharon Lanciani, Boston MA

Sarah Langton-Lockton, CAE, London

Brian Mackey, Irish Linen Museum

Paul McDonough, Boston, MA

Trevor Mitchell, English Heritage

Kate Morgan, Castle Howard

Oliver Green, Colchester Castle Museum

Anne Jones, Farnham Museum

Jeffery Lord, ADAPT

Anthony Pilling, Lancashire County Council

Vincent Pool, Rochdale Borough Council

John Preston, Conservation and Design Officer, Cambridge

Alan Richards, DOE

Tristan Rees Roberts, Freeland Rees Roberts, Cambridge

Andrew Rolfe, Burnley Borough Council

David Shatwell, Butress Fuller Alsop Practice, Manchester

Leslie Simpson, Down County Museum

Michael Stanton, FAIA, San Francisco

Jessica Sutcliffe, Square Chapel Trust

Stephen Thorpe, Threshold Architects

Andrew Walker, Architectural Association

Valerie Wenham, Disability Advisor, The National Trust

John Worthington, IOAAS, York

ILLUSTRATION CREDITS

1

A
PATTERN
OF CHANGE

WHAT IS DISABLED ACCESS?

'Disabled access' is a phrase generally used to refer to ramped access for wheelchair users. This ungrammatical usage is still part of our lexicon today and routinely shows up on architectural drawings and in our discussions. Despite its common usage, the perception of disability is changing. The access movement has broadened public perception and understanding beyond the narrow definition that wheelchair users are the only disabled people. Disabled access has become a catalyst for improving physical access for all building users, including ambulant people 'disabled' as a result of age, temporary injury or illness, people with sensory impairments and parents with young children.

Disability has been interpreted as a minority issue affecting a stereotypical consumer. The reality is that disability is endemic to the human condition. From the cradle to the grave we are all materially incapacitated by our surroundings in what are totally predictable and inevitable circumstances, whether as children, in pregnancy, as parents with children, in old age, or as a result of accident or illness, congenital defect or inherited characteristic.

In environmental terms disability is experienced as inability to negotiate what is in effect a purpose-built environment created to meet the needs of the ultimate, stereotype 'modular man' – male, able-bodied and independent. This effectively restricts our own independence, deprives us of the valuable participation or company of others and negates any concept of equal opportunity. Those of us who may not consider ourselves disabled because we do not currently rely on the recognizable trappings of the physically disabled – the wheelchair, the Zimmer frame, the white cane, or the hearing aid – must realize that the ageing process will gradually and imperceptibly limit our ability to function in this stereotypical environment.

While we are, of course, encouraged to prepare financially for our old age, there is also surely a moral imperative for society to prepare environmentally, in order that we may have independence at that time, irrespective of currently fashionable political or financial considerations.[1]

King's College Library, Cambridge

This is the lesson from the 'access' works at King's College Library, Cambridge. Wheelchair users and other disabled people are the incidental beneficiaries of a scheme designed to improve overall access to library and dining facilities on the upper floors of the College Library. In 1992 architects, Freeland Rees Roberts, Cambridge, designed a new scheme to replace the existing staircase with a passenger lift and new stone staircase. This type of improvement could be used by students and staff, including older College tutors, who preferred or required lift access over the existing staircase.

The original library building was designed by William Wilkins in a style described by Pevsner as the 'collegiate Gothicism of Cambridge'.[2] The Library was completed as part of a new range of buildings added to the college between 1824 and 1828. Later alterations and additions to the range of buildings beginning in 1927 allowed the Library to expand thereby changing Wilkins' original approach and circulation into the Library building and upper floors. Figure 1.1(a) shows the existing entrance arrangement with the external steps leading through an open portal to form the interior staircase which existed when Freeland Rees Roberts planned their scheme.

The 1992 scheme removed the existing staircase and replaced it with a new staircase and passenger lift. Figure 1.1(a) also shows the entrance portal after alteration, now forming an enclosed doorway leading to a new lift lobby and stairwell. This required removal of the external steps and modification to the portal opening to form a doorway which now provides level access into the new lift and staircase lobby area. In order to obtain the necessary space for the new lift lobby and lift shaft where the old staircase had been, the existing walls were reduced in thickness to increase available floor area. Stonework for the modified doorway is carefully matched to the original, but the new work serves as a reminder of the earlier configuration of the steps; the new – fully interior – staircase is finished in limestone; the handrails are wrought iron; both stone and iron work are in keeping with the collegiate gothic character of

1.1 King's College Library, Cambridge.

1.1 (a) Library entrance before and after alteration.

1.1 (b) In some areas of the library wheelchair access is not possible; new handrails and contrasting nosings were added for safety and to ease circulation.

1.1 (c) Interior view of new stone staircase around the lift shaft.

(a)

(b)

(c)

the buildings in this range (Figure 1.1(c)). The slender iron railings were added to other existing staircases, along with contrasting nosings (Figure 1.1(b)), improvements which specifically benefit disabled people with limited vision or limited mobility but which also improve circulation and safety for all users.

The historical ambience of the new stairwell has been enhanced by the re-use of fanciful stone ornamentation which the College had removed during earlier exterior stone repair work to other College buildings. The result is an elegant and historically sympathetic alteration which provides access for wheelchair users and others in an integrated setting appropriate to the building's special architectural interest and collegiate context.

EQUAL TREATMENT VS SPECIAL TREATMENT

The basic objective of access is to secure easy and dignified circulation for all users in and around a site, building or other structure, and to provide access to toilets and other public areas. Dignified access for disabled people comes from enjoying independent movement and integrated circulation. Independent movement means freedom from being carried or having to rely on assistance to move about or to find the way. Integrated access allows all visitors and building users, whether able-bodied or not, to use the same route throughout. Meeting these objectives minimizes the stigma attached to disability, and reduces the segregation, frustration and disappointment disabled people can experience when they cannot get to or find where they need to be.

The reason that access to historic buildings sometimes provokes a negative response from conservationists is that it brings new moral and ethical issues to the conservation goal of preserving architectural and historic integrity. This has been highlighted by the comment of one English Heritage inspector:

For many years conservationists occupied a moral high ground on which their wish to preserve historic buildings from alteration was usually seen as a worthy objective in the public interest, whereas those who wished to alter historic buildings were frequently viewed as self interested and motivated by the prospect of private (usually financial) gain. Now the moral high ground is also occupied by people who have a new set of equally worthy objectives acknowledged to be in the public interest. Their objectives often conflict with the accepted views of the conservation movement, and the pressure to meet them often puts conservationists on the defensive.[3]

Opinions tend to divide on questions of how and where. This raises a fundamental question as to what standards of access are appropriate and indeed necessary for the historic environment.

In 1983 Selwyn Goldsmith, author of *Designing for the Disabled* examined the source of social considerations behind the standard of integrated and independent access:

The contention is that the differences observable in the UK and US approaches to designing for the disabled stem from two distinctive cultural ethics regarding societal treatment of disabled people ... An analysis of opposing cultural values indicates that a coherent ideology for designing for the disabled could only have evolved in the self-help culture of the United States. Commentaries on the genesis of the [self-help] movement confirm a doctrine of normalisation and independence ...[4]

Normalization and independence mean that for a person with disabilities there is no scent of patronage, condescension, charity or philanthropy. In design terms it means *independence* and not reliance on help or attendants; *integration* and the avoidance of segregated routes.

Meeting the goals of independence and integration can present the biggest hurdle for improving access to historic buildings. Although we may look for solutions which achieve integration and independence for all people, when these include the provision of level access for wheelchair users, the alterations may adversely affect the special historic interest of the building or site. The installation of an access ramp or wheelchair platform lift at a principal entrance, which would harm significant architectural features or affect the harmonious balance of the façade, may well not be approved, regardless of the social, ethical or political justification for integrated access. Appreciating when it is acceptable to make a compromise solution is as important as knowing how to execute the design and details for new ramps and handrails.

The access objectives of independence and integration are embraced in many of the case studies and examples in this book. Chapter Three on circulation strategies illustrates the range of strategies possible for historic buildings: altering the principal entrance, finding a new public entrance, finding a suitable side door entrance and using a temporary ramp. Why a compromise solution is necessary is explained. Chapter Four looks at specific design issues, affecting the approach to the building and the design and detailing of new elements, ramps and handrails. Chapter Five focuses on vertical circulation strategies, considering the conservation constraints for introducing mechanical lift devices into historic properties. The focus in the final chapter is on cultural monuments: roofed and unroofed scheduled ancient monuments and country houses. These studies are illustrated in a separate chapter because the visitor circulation strategies involve less intervention and physical alteration than those designed for public working buildings like the studies drawn from civic buildings such as town halls and libraries, or commercial buildings.

The schemes illustrated in Chapter Six show that access should not be looked at in isolation. The use of the historic building or site must be considered, together with the type of people likely to visit the property and, most importantly, whether it will be for their employment, commercial use or leisure pursuit. Just as the needs of a person vary by disability and degree of disability, the way the property is used or can be used, must be considered. The stately homes of the National Trust and many private estates and unroofed and roofed monument sites maintained by English Heritage will have different access needs to an eighteenth-century chapel which may be converted to a performing arts centre (like The Square Chapel, Halifax, discussed in Chapter Three).

The access checklist or audit is a useful resource to identify the existing physical and communication barriers for a variety of disabilities. However, the physical audit is only part of the process. It is also necessary to undertake an organizational audit to identify the way the building is used or could be used to meet the access needs, and to assess which features contribute to the building's special architectural or historic interest. A barrier such as the stepped access to the first floor may be an important architectural feature which cannot be altered. A way of avoiding the barrier rather than making an alteration to it may therefore be necessary. The skill and creative objective of an access assessment for a historic property is to consider the ways in which barriers can be overcome without alteration by planning alternative circulation routes. When intervention is unavoidable, the assessment should devise a sensitive and appropriate design scheme to alter existing features without diminishing the special architectural or historic interest.

Ultimately, the objective must be to find a solution which disabled people can easily use. There are many examples of alterations which provide 'access' but in a way not readily useable. A notable example comes from Boston, Massachusetts, at Faneuil Hall, a National Historic Landmark dating from 1742. Some of the most important meetings in the history of the American Revolutionary Movement took place in the public hall on the first floor. Today the hall serves as a meeting area and museum. An original plan provided for two mechanical devices, one at the entrance and a second for vertical circulation. The entrance lift is a unique telescopic hydraulic lift which rises up out of the cobble paving in front of the entrance and then telescopes out and over three steps to the level of the threshold at the entrance, providing wheelchair access into the building (Figure 1.2(a)). Once inside, a platform lift carries the wheelchair users up two flights of steps to the public hall. A few years

1.2 Faneuil Hall, Boston, Massachusetts.

1.2 (*a*) The telescopic lift originally used at the entrance facing Quincy Market. The original town hall meeting building was erected in 1742 and takes it name from the wealthy merchant, Peter Faneuil, who built it at his own expense. It originally included a market hall on the ground floor and a meeting hall on the upper floors. The original building was gutted by fire in 1763, which destroyed all but the brick walls. After rebuilding, it became associated with the patriot leaders and earned the title 'Cradle of Liberty'.

1.2 (*b*) Side elevation showing the original window (third bay) before alteration to form doorway.

1.2 (*c*) Side elevation showing the same window after a doorway was formed. The new side opening leads to a passenger lift.

(*See page* 5.)

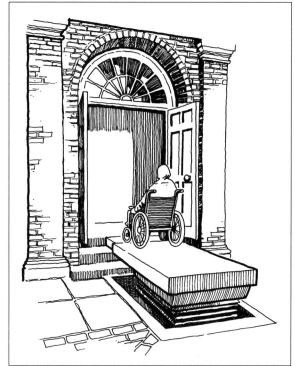

(*a*)

(*b*)

(*c*)

later these devices were proving unworkable and were replaced with a more integrated design solution, the passenger lift (Figure 1.2(b) and (c)). Since a fundamental conservation principle is to avoid unnecessary change, access solutions must be workable. If the interests of conservation must be balanced against the interests of access, change which benefits the most users makes more sense than alterations which serve wheelchair users alone, who are a minority of the population.

The key to reaching an acceptable compromise is to assess the limitations and opportunities at each site. Then, taking account of its unique architectural and historic interest, put these limitations and opportunities in the context of the varying access needs, depending on the building or site's intended use and the circulation needs for the public and staff. Just as an audit of the existing circulation may reveal stepped vertical access, an audit of the conservation barriers may reveal historic floor beams which cannot be modified to install a passenger lift (see discussion of King's Manor).

WHY MAKE ANY IMPROVEMENT AT ALL?

Building conservation is one means of preserving the historic, aesthetic, scientific and social value of our physical cultural heritage for future generations. Historic value is the association we make between a place and a historic figure, event, phase or activity. For buildings of architectural interest, it is the aesthetic or design value or authorship that may be most important. Other places may have archaeological, scientific or research value. Cultural monuments, in particular, may have social value and be a focus of our spiritual, political, national or other cultural expression.

The authenticity of a surviving historic place is fundamental to the values we associate with historic environment:

> For any given place the significance will be greater where evidence of the association or event survives *in situ*, or where the settings are substantially intact, than where it

has been changed or evidence does not survive.[6]

This statement from the *Guidelines to the Burra Charter* embodies the long-held conservation principle behind the practice of minimal intervention. Any one of the protected values of a resource can be lost if the authenticity of the place is diminished through unsuitable alteration or demolition. Other accepted practices aim to protect authenticity through the preservation of original fabric, reversibility of alterations, and the avoidance of restoration. If, as a result of decay or destruction, restoration is needed, new work should respect the historic and artistic work of the past, rather than reproduce the original in every respect.[7]

> Generally speaking, authenticity is ascribed to a heritage resource that is materially original or genuine (as it was constructed) and as it has aged and changed in time. Its historic authenticity should reflect the significant phases of construction and utilization in the different periods of its historic time line.[8]

The concept of each building or site having its own 'time line' is explained this way by Dr Jokilehto:

> The relationship of a heritage resource, such as a work of art, a historic building, or an historic town, with time and history reflects three significant periods of construction and utilization:
>
> (a)   the first period that results in the creation;
>
> (b)   the second period that extends from the end of its creation period to present time;
>
> (c)   the third period that is associated with the perception of the monument in our consciousness at present time.[9]

This link with specific historical periods becomes a fundamental reference for the evaluation of an historic resource, with the specific periods providing a reference to the artistic and social trends of its creation period and a basis for evaluation of how the resource contributed to those trends.

(a)

(b)

1.3 King's Manor, York.

1.3 (a) The front elevation shows the age and character of the structure.

1.3 (b) Anti-chamber to the Huntingdon Room. On the advice of English Heritage, the University conducted a limited opening up of the floor to study the structure in the area where the lift shaft was proposed, before proceeding with an application for listed building consent. This revealed ancient fabric which was unsuitable to remove or alter for the purposes of adding a lift in the area.

The Institute of Advanced Architectural Studies of the University of York occupies the King's Manor (Figure 1.3), the former Abbot's House adjacent to St Mary's Abbey, in the City of York. The House as it survives today is mostly a re-building of the late fifteenth century although surviving thirteenth-century stonework can be found on the lower elevations.[5] The former Council Chamber on the first floor of the medieval range is now the Huntingdon Room and serves as public lecture and conference space. These first floor rooms are reached via an important historic stone staircase from the seventeenth century. The Huntingdon room links horizontally to dining facilities, often also used during conferences. The Institute desired a solution for vertical access for wheelchair users to the first floor rooms in the two wings. One option was to add a wheelchair platform lift to the historic staircase. Institute management preferred the option of a passenger lift, since this would meet the needs of people with other types of disability and could be used by others who preferred lift access, including the catering staff serving conference functions.

The initial location identified for the passenger lift was adjacent to the historic staircase. A meeting with the York City Council conservation officer and the English Heritage Historic Buildings Adviser was convened before an application for listed building consent was prepared. This pre-application meeting gave the Institute and conservation officials an opportunity to review the options for improving vertical access. English Heritage suggested that the Institute conduct a limited opening-up to inspect the existing floor timbers at the preferred location for the passenger lift, before proceeding with a full planning application. When this was done, early original floor beams forming the original structural members were found where the proposed lift shaft would have been, a *conservation* barrier to access.

This sequence of periods also helps explain the period of creation and use buildings or sites undergo. All buildings and sites are the product of the specific cultural, social, economic and political conditions of the periods that contributed to their creation, evolution and usage.

For some buildings or sites – or some parts – there will be little or no further adaptation or change. Works are restricted to repair and maintenance of the historic fabric. Often these buildings or sites will have ceased to have economic value; they are preserved in the present time for their interpretative value and historical associations to people, events and time periods. Other buildings and sites are continuing to evolve and will undergo a constant process of adaptation, as they continue in use or are put to new and changing uses. Health and safety regulations relating to public occupation have changed over time and have been just one of the factors contributing to this process of adaptation. Accessibility requirements can be viewed as another factor contributing to this process.

The process of adaptation at historic properties is permitted in part to keep the building or structure in use so it will not become neglected and fall into disrepair. How much a building or structure continues to evolve, forms one basis for the distinction between working buildings and cultural monuments, and the differing approaches towards their repair and upkeep.[10]

In the day-to-day management of the historic environment, the concepts of historic time line and authenticity can help explain the differences in decisions made about alterations to historic buildings, including the appropriateness of access alterations to a particular building or site.

A *pattern of change*

The Departments of National Heritage and the Department of Environment published Planning and Policy Guidance Note 15 (PPG 15) in September 1994.[11] The purpose of the guidance is to provide pragmatic advice on the application of established conservation principles to the way in which works to historic buildings and development within a conservation area should be undertaken. It is relevant to both those directly engaged in such works and to others, for example local planning authorities and English Heritage, who are involved in assessing such proposals. It starts, naturally enough, with a strong statement on the value of sound conservation practices:

> The physical survivals of our past are to be valued for their own sake, as a central part of our cultural heritage and our sense of national identity. They are an irreplaceable record which contributes through formal education and in many other ways, to our understanding of both the present and the past …[12]

One of the values of PPG 15 is that it relates conservation to other objectives. Conservation must be balanced with other national policies which promote sustainable and viable economic growth. PPG 15 recognizes that there are few occasions when it is possible to preserve a building unchanged.

> Generally the best way of securing the upkeep of historic buildings and areas is to keep them in active use. For the great majority this must mean economically viable uses if they are to survive, and new and even continuing uses will often necessitate some degree of adaptation. The range and acceptability of possible uses must therefore usually be a major consideration when the future of a listed building or buildings in conservation areas is in question.[13]

Most historic buildings have some use as a place of home, a place of employment, a location for civic and commercial uses, or a place for leisure or cultural activities. These are working buildings. Their cultural value may be separate from the type of function which takes place at the building or site. For the majority of these buildings, the capacity to accommodate change and adaptation is an essential part of keeping them in use. Intervention into their fabric or setting may be kept to a minimum to preserve their authenticity and special interest, yet conservation principles accommodate some alteration as a means of ensuring their continued preservation and repair.

Cultural monuments are different. These may include Scheduled Ancient Monuments, listed buildings and other historic buildings and structures. While a Grade I or Grade II* listing (Grade A or B in Scotland) may reflect a building's particular value, vernacular and other modest Grade II buildings may have rarity value as surviving examples of periods of building and be treated as cultural 'monuments' although of humble origin.

For cultural monuments, their particular special interest is the key factor which draws visitors. Their ancient or rare fabric may be studied or enjoyed as a record of social development and historical change, rather than as a setting for contemporary uses as with working buildings. Their fabric is protected from adverse change by legislation. However, unlike working buildings, alterations will not generally be necessary to preserve the building or monument. Their economic value, with a few exceptions, is minimal. These buildings are of such cultural importance that their continued survival is maintained through public or private support as opposed to economic use:

> If a building is so sensitive that it cannot sustain any alterations to keep it in viable economic use, its future may nevertheless be secured by charitable or community ownership preserved for its own sake for local people and for the visiting public, where possible with non-destructive uses. Many listed buildings subsist successfully in this way – from the great houses of the National Trust to buildings such as guildhalls, churches and windmills cared for by local authorities or trusts ...[14]

For working buildings, occupation and use is the most universally accepted method to ensure their preservation and maintenance. The continuation of the use for which a building was originally erected generally requires fewer changes than when a new use is contemplated. However, when continuation of the original use is not feasible, new uses may provide the means of preservation, if compatible with the particular interest of the building or site.

Changes in the use and structure of historic buildings were going on long before the access debate emerged. For many industrial buildings, their original functions may have ceased altogether; newer buildings accommodating modern-day operations require conversion in order to avoid the problems of disuse, destruction and decay. In addition to industrial buildings, many town halls have been through such a process. This process of change and adaptation continues:

> New uses may often be the key to a building's or area's preservation, and controls ... should be exercised sympathetically where this would enable a historic building or area to be given a new lease of life ... Patterns of economic activity inevitably change over time ...[15]

The United Church, Winchester

Demolition of the existing Grade II* Victorian church on a prominent city site in Winchester was one option considered by the Congregational Church, which now occupies the Winchester Congregational Chapel.[16] The church needed to expand its facilities and required a more visible, street-level presence as it assumed a larger community role: a small chapel opening directly off the street, an office and counselling room, foyer and coffee-bar with good public visibility *and* access for wheelchair users and older visitors. The church building dates from 1853, and is situated between two wings of the Old Gaol, earlier buildings dating from 1805. The existing entrance, raised some two metres above street level, has proved to be a barrier to both wheelchair users and others who could not negotiate steps, as well as enclosing church functions away from the public (Figure 1.4).

An 1852 edition of the *Illustrated Exhibitor and Magazine of Art* describes the chapel as an important departure from the previous style of chapel buildings for independent churches: 'A pleasing change has taken place from the dull heavy brick buildings with square windows, and ordinary house doors, destitute of pediment, porch or pillar.' (Figure 1.4(a)). The chapel roof is supported by eighteen slender fluted stone columns with moulded arches, and a cast iron front gallery. The unusual

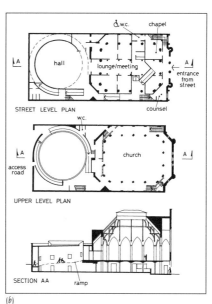

STREET LEVEL PLAN

UPPER LEVEL PLAN

SECTION AA

(a)

(b)

1.4 United Church, Winchester.

1.4 (a) Front elevation before alteration.

1.4 (b) Section, ground and upper floor plans.

1.4 (c) Front elevation after alteration.

1.4 (d) Interior view of the Chapel after alteration (photograph: Joe Low).

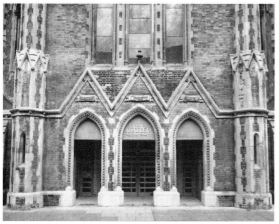

(c)

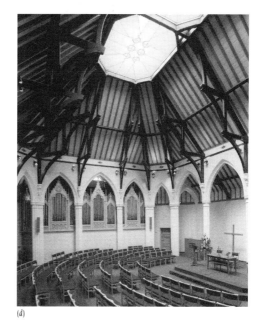

(d)

height of the chapel provided the opportunity to raise the floor level without compromising the architectural features or original intent. Architects plb architecture (formerly Plincke, Leaman & Browning) describe the space released at ground level by raising the first floor, as a new undercroft for the expanded public facilities needed by the congregation to continue use of the building (Figure 1.4(b)). This links to a new circular meeting hall added to the rear of the church. At the front entrance the existing steps were removed and existing solid doors replaced with a glass screen set back into the façade to encourage visitors and to provide level access without disturbing the essential feel of the building (Figure 1.4(c)).

While raising the floor level provided the means of adapting the building to new uses, lift access to the new upper-level church was considered inappropriate as a means of access for worship, weddings and funerals; a staircase without a lift would not work for disabled people. The solution was a circular ramp from street level which wraps around the new circular hall leading to the Chapel now on a mezzanine floor level. Access to the ramp is also possible directly from street level to the rear of the meeting hall.

Acceptance of a radical scheme of this type does not typify English Heritage's normal policy on alterations to maintain a historic building in use. It demonstrates that there may be greater flexibility if schemes secure the preservation of essential features which contribute to the building's special architectural interest.

A *changed use*: Scottish Fisheries Museum, Anstruther, Scotland

The museum is housed in a group of former domestic buildings located around three sides of a cobbled courtyard. The buildings are historically and geographically associated with the fishing industry in Scotland and provided an ideal home to the award-winning Scottish Fisheries Museum (Figure 1.5). Surviving structures such as the Abbots Lodge date from the sixteenth century. Other dwellings include eighteenth-century cottages

and a mid-nineteenth-century store-house. The fisherman's cottage retains its domestic layout to form part of the historical and social interpretation of fishing life, while other buildings have been adapted internally to accommodate different galleries covering the diverse and ancillary aspects of the fishing industry. Recently the museum acquired an adjacent boatyard to house its collection of small historic vessels which form the basis of a new exhibition.

A general refurbishment of the premises and upgrade of the collections provided the opportunity to plan a level route of access for wheelchair users which could also be used by the many parents with children in prams and pushchairs. Visitors enter the museum through the main entrance which is ramped from the pavement to the level of the courtyard. Through the courtyard visitors enter the converted historic dwellings. The entire visitor circulation route is a gently sloping ramp connecting floor levels and the individual structures.

Buildings like the King's College Library at Cambridge, the United Church in Winchester and the converted dwellings which now form the Scottish Fisheries Museum demonstrate the successful resolution of a diversity of access issues in the context of historic buildings. The different approaches and degree of intervention attest to the need for site-specific solutions, which take account of conservation constraints, the use of the property and the unique opportunities individual properties offer.

CONSERVATION GUIDANCE

Neither international charters nor the existing national heritage legislation are recent enough to provide express statements of the needs of disabled people (see note 10); thus they provide no direct guidance on the ethical dilemma of access and conservation. Being more recent, there was the opportunity to include in Planning and Policy Guidance Note 15 a basic policy statement to inform decisions on access proposals. The standard adopted is one which aims to achieve a minimum level of dignity for the user while respecting the building's special interest:

'It is important in principle that disabled people should have dignified easy access to and within historic buildings. If it is treated as part of an integrated review of access requirements for all visitors or users, and a flexible and pragmatic approach is taken, it should normally be possible to plan suitable access for disabled people without compromising a building's special

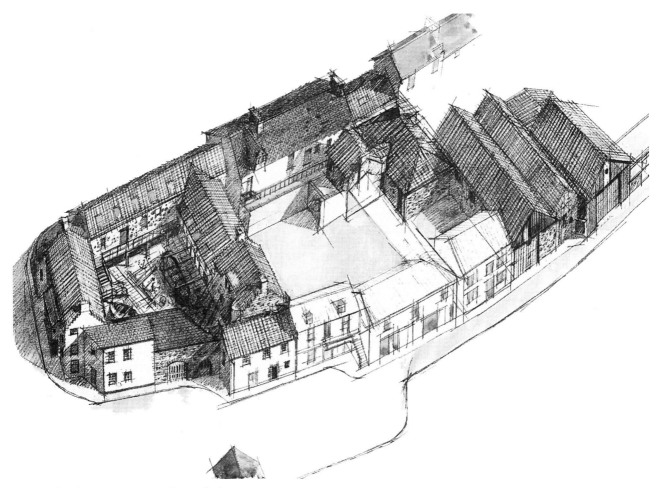

1.5 Scottish Fisheries Museum, Anstruther, Scotland.

The principal part of the museum is housed in an interesting group of historic and architecturally important buildings converted from domestic use but historically associated with the fishing industry. The museum has now expanded into the adjacent boatyard. One of the more controversial alterations to the domestic dwellings was the addition of an internal link between the upper floors which is shown in the upper left-hand corner of the courtyard area. The museum desired this link between buildings to overcome the previous vertical circulation via existing internal staircases of the two adjacent dwellings.

interest. Alternative routes or re-organising the use of spaces may achieve the desired result without the need for damaging alterations.'[17]

Norwich public inquiry

Shortly after PPG 15 was published, PPG section 3.28 was cited in evidence both as support and opposition by the parties to a public inquiry involving a dispute over a proposed access ramp to a listed banking building, occupied by National Westminster Bank located in the city centre conservation area of Norwich (Figure 1.6). The 1924 banking building by F. C. R. Palmer and W. F. C. Holden features neo-classical ornamentation: a pillared portico and, in Pevsner's words, the 'somewhat Wrenian turret and cupola'. The building is prominently located at the sharp corner of two city centre streets, within the city conservation area.

The scheme for the addition of an access ramp to the front elevation illustrates the inherent difficulties and complexities of designing both for independence and integration in the historic context (Figure 1.6(b)). The dispute over the scheme also demonstrates the need for local authorities to reconcile access policies, which, for political reasons, rightly promote front door access schemes with the policies of conservation and planning departments.

The appeal arose following the planning decision of Norwich council not to grant listed building consent to the proposed ramp. National Westminster Bank had applied to Norwich City Council for planning permission and listed building consent for an access ramp to the main entrance. The entrance is approached via a short flight of semi-circular steps. The ramp would have risen from the level of the pavement along the side elevation and turned the corner, cutting into part of the steps which are a prominent feature. The diagonal line of the proposed ramp is emphasized by the handrails which would have cut across the existing decorative metal work. The appeal's inspector concluded that the diagonal line cut by the ramp and

(a)

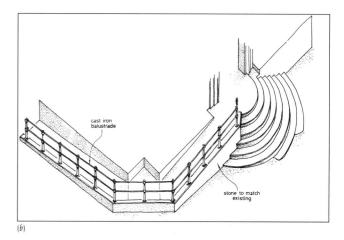

(b)

1.6 National Westminster Bank, Norwich.

1.6 (a) Front elevation.

1.6 (b) View of the proposed access ramp based on the drawings the Bank submitted with its application for listed building consent. The Bank attempted to argue that the existing sloping site, causing the steps to be non-symmetrical, had already impacted on the building façade. The inspector noted the asymmetry of the steps but disagreed with the Bank's argument that the steps unbalanced the overall classical proportions of the façade so that a further asymmetrical element would not affect the character of the building.

handrails would unbalance the architectural composition of this prominent city centre building.

The inspector characterized the proposed ramp and handrails as 'visual clutter' and judged they would unbalance the symmetry of the neo-classical façade. On this basis the inspector upheld the Council's refusal of listed building consent. The basis for the decision is that for a building where aspects of symmetry and balance contribute to its special architectural interest, new elements such as the proposed slope of the ramp – which do not harmonize with the existing design and which could potentially unbalance the classical façade – should not be permitted. (Some of the design solutions for harmonizing ramps into classical elevations are discussed in Chapter Four.)

The inspector also found that the building's architectural interest contributed to the surrounding conservation area, so the proposed ramp to the front entrance would affect the setting as well as the building. This was cited as a second, and separate basis for denial of listed building consent.

This is an important decision since it demonstrates that if one of the special interests of the building is the design value of its symmetrical façade, and if an access ramp would have a negative impact on the design – even if there is minimum impact on the structure or fabric, or it is reversible – the scheme is unacceptable. As the opinion notes it 'was of no consequence' that the ramp would be constructed independently of the existing structure because it abuts the plinth and for all intents and purposes would be a permanent feature and read as a continuous structure.

Alternative locations

One other factor which contributed to the refusal of listed building consent was the availability of the banking service at other branches located in the city centre. National Westminster Bank would not commit themselves to these branches remaining open, or being made accessible. The opinion suggests that the availability of alternative locations for the delivery of services should be considered as an alternative to applying for consent to make a potentially harmful alteration to a building of architectural importance, and which contributes to the city centre conservation area.

Burnley Central Library, Lancashire

New access works at the Burnley Central Library illustrate a very different approach which was approved for a city centre area. The ramp is a radical departure from the original stepped access. In plan the ramp is a new asymmetrical feature which sweeps in front of the building across the façade (Figure 1.7).

The existing library building dates from 1929 to 1930 and was designed by Arthur Race, the Borough Engineer and Surveyor. Pevsner describes the design as 'Beaux-Arts classicism, with an entrance loggia with two giant columns.' It is located in a small square opposite the neo-classical-styled Police Station and Magistrate Courts.

The design of the new ramp makes a radical change to the appearance and especially the setting of the building. The justification for such intervention was the way the new ramp provides a beneficial facelift to a part of the city otherwise suffering from the effects of post-industrial economic decline after its heyday as an important textile town in the early twentieth century. Details of the scheme record this history, with the new stone and iron works which decorate the ramp featuring carvings and hand wrought motifs taken from the mills (Figure 1.7(c)). The provision of seating in front of the curved podium walls of the ramp and on the raised podium were intended to bring people into the area, creating a new urban focal point and a new point of architectural and urban interest. Continuing the tradition of civic-designed architecture, the scheme is by the Lancashire County Council Design and Development Group.

Reassessment and new progress: County Down Museum, Northern Ireland

One of the many challenges of getting access right is keeping up with the pace of change as the access movement matures and

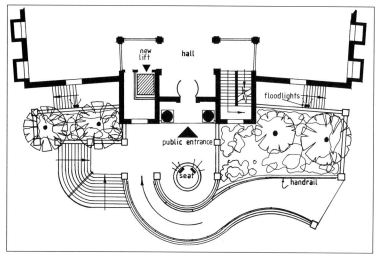

(a)

1.7 Burnley Central Library, Lancashire.

1.7 (a) Plan showing the new steps, ramp and seating area at the front elevation which replaced a steep flight of steps leading from the main entrance.

1.7 (b) Front elevation after alteration.

1.7 (c) Detail of hand-carved work in the stone base of the new ramp. The stonework and decorative iron railings was partly grant-aided by the Arts Council.

(*See page* 15.)

(b)

(c)

as concepts like integrated and independent access become the norm. The changing definition of who disabled people are, and a growing awareness of disability has prompted a new look at existing access schemes to see what more can be done to meet the needs of disabled people and others not traditionally considered disabled.

At the County Down Museum, staff are considering again whether it is possible to overcome the limited access to one of the principal buildings which forms a significant part of the site and which houses important collections.

The museum occupies the converted prison of the old Down County Gaol built between 1789 and 1796 (Figure 1.8). The

Gatehouse, the Governor's residence (where the gaoler used to live) and the Cell block (with surviving interior cells from the eighteenth century) are the most complete surviving Irish gaol of their type and period (Figure 1.8(c)).

When the site was first converted, finding a suitable means of access into and around the Governor's house seemed impossible because of the historic and architectural interest of the building and the potential impact external alterations would

(a)

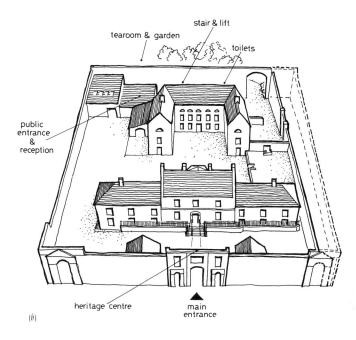

(b)

(c)

1.8 County Down Museum, Northern Ireland.

1.8 (a) View through the Gatehouse showing the steps up to the Governor's House which houses the principal part of the museum displays.

1.8 (b) Site plan showing the museum site which includes the Gatehouse, Governor's residence and the Cell block. A gentle regrading of the footway leading to the Gatehouse entrance provides level access into the Museum complex. There is also level access into the historic Cell block. A new addition to rear of the Cell block provides lift access to educational rooms and staff offices.

1.8 (c) Cell block: narrow corridors through the eighteenth century cells restrict wheelchair access. The museum provides a narrow wheelchair for those able to transfer; for others unable to view the cells, it is possible to gain a sense of the environment by leaving the doors ajar.

(See page 15.)

have on the overall setting. Consequently the museum had to accept there would be no access for people who could not negotiate steps. This was also true of an exhibit in the first floor of the Gatehouse.

Today, museum staff are re-examining the options for lift access into the building and for circulation, as part of the ongoing process of improving access for visitors as funds become available and as attitudes towards access change.

Is *access an issue?*

When English Heritage published its *Guidance Note, Easy Access to Historic Properties*, in October 1995, it made clear that improving access is a legitimate conservation objective. This is recorded in the policy statement:

English Heritage seeks to ensure that its programmes and activities are accessible to everyone, wherever practicable. It aims to provide easy and dignified access to its own estate whenever this can be reasonably done, and encourages others who own or manage historic properties to adopt access plans which are consistent with the special architectural, historic or archaeological character of the property concerned.[19]

It is fair to say that the debate about *whether* to make access improvements has settled down. The challenge now lies, and perhaps always has, with the how and the where, and to what degree. These questions are explored through the case studies in the chapters that follow.

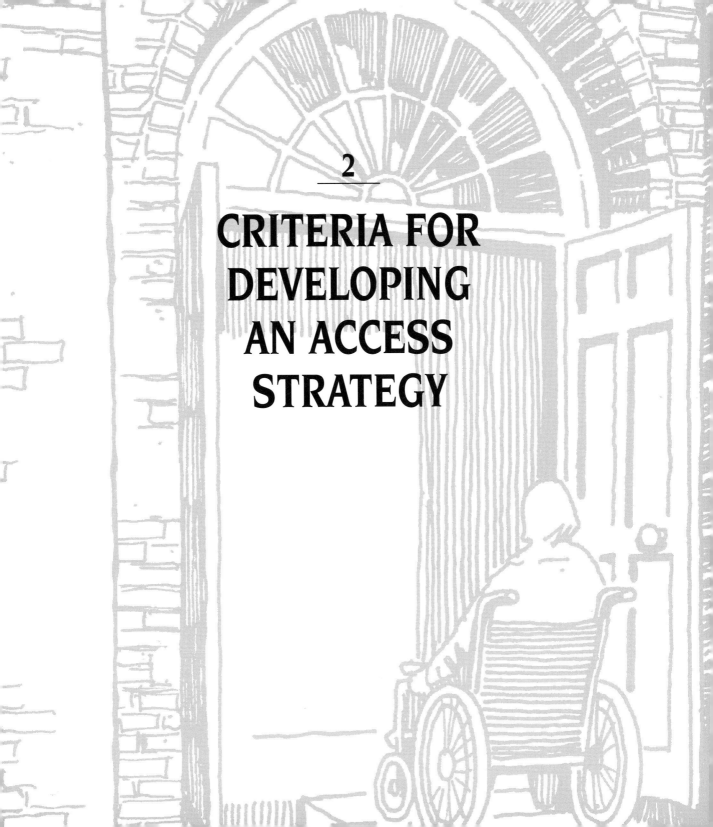

2

CRITERIA FOR DEVELOPING AN ACCESS STRATEGY

Access checklist

Step 1: Identify your access needs

What are the activities held in the building or site? Is it a place of business, of public service, or is it a cultural monument?

Who uses the property, and how is it used? Are the needs of the staff the same as those of visitors?

Is the need for access long term or short term? Is the need continuous or occasional?

What are the future plans for the uses of the property? Are there any changes or building works proposed?

Where are the barriers to access? Are they physical or communicational barriers?

What is the view of disabled users and local access groups? What is the view of the local authority access officer?

Step 2: Consider whether access can be provided in ways that avoid alterations to the building

Is there an organisational change that will overcome access difficulties without loss of dignity? Can the use be achieved in a way that avoids or minimises access difficulties?

• relocating a public function, for example from the first floor to the ground floor, may make it accessible without damaging alterations

• adjusting the circulation route may avoid obstacles, such as stepped thesholds, narrow doors, etc

• making use of printed literature and technology to provide and present information may enable a person with disabilities to use a service without actually visiting the building

Consider access needs before acquiring a property that is unsuitable for the intended use.

Generally

Ensure that any access proposals will meet the need. If the scheme does not meet the need, or is difficult to use, the alterations will have been in vain.

Ensure that permission is obtained for any alterations to protected properties. Ensure that access solutions conform to conservation principles.

Step 3: If some alteration is still necessary consider the following

Is the property listed, scheduled, in a conservation area, or in a registered historic park or garden? What is the cultural significance of the building? (It is sensible to discuss this with the local authority conservation officer.)

• determine the importance of the site or building's design in its protected status

• work out what is sensitive about the fabric of the site or building

• avoid proposals that would have an adverse effect on the historic or architectural interest or setting of the property

How does the layout and form of the building influence the proposals?

• evaluate the ways into the building and how the internal circulation system could be linked to an entrance which is accessible or which can be altered

• identify areas of the building which are capable of alteration due to previous changes or to the lack of sensitive fabric

Do the proposals meet the long term pattern of use for the building? Are they of sufficient quality to contribute to the cultural value of the building?

What is the view of the local authority conservation officer?

2.1 **English Heritage Access Checklist.**

The English Heritage Access Checklist provides one example of a framework for pulling together the information necessary to develop an access strategy for a historic property (Figure 2.1).

An access scheme must both meet the needs of the users and preserve, respect or enhance a building or site's special architectural or historic interest. The English Heritage Guidance Note sets out a suggested process to make an access assessment for a historic building or site, as part of the process of developing an overall access strategy to accomplish these objectives. This is summarized in Figure 2.1, bringing together the various parts of the equation and forming a framework for the need for new works. This provides the basis for developing an access strategy, which can become part of the action plan for the property.

An access assessment process gathers information on the following issues:

- Identification of access needs:
  - What are the accessibility legal requirements under the Disability Discrimination Act of 1995 and other statutory or advisory guidance?
  - What is the need for access, including the existing and desired level of provision of access?
  - What are the existing physical and communication barriers?
- Consideration of existing organizational and administrative practices which could be changed or modified to avoid or minimize alterations:
  -- Is access part of a change of use or feasibility study for re-use of the building?
- Consideration of the conservation factors if alterations are necessary:
  - What are the long-term use requirements of the building or site?
  - What factors can be used to evaluate the potential impact of alterations or demolitions to historic fabric or the setting?

The information produced from an access assessment can then be used to develop an access strategy specific to the building or structure and its setting. The Access Committee for England recommends that building owners use the access assessment process to develop action plans for their properties.

ACTION PLANS

An action plan is a strategy and programme for removing or working around physical barriers in premises where goods or services are provided over a period of time. Having an effective action plan can reduce the potential for successful complaint against the service provider by removing causes for complaint over time, by demonstrating to disabled people that the service provider is already taking achievable measures to ensure equality of treatment and by providing targets and bench-marks for measuring progress.

Components of an action plan:
- **an access audit of the premises and site;**
- **consultation with disabled users in deciding priorities;**
- **preparation of a programme and timetable for implementation of the programme;**
- **a review procedure.**

This chapter starts with a summary of the legal requirements under the Disability Discrimination Act and other legislation, followed by a summary of conservation factors. The final section sets out the minimum dimensions and other criteria to evaluate circulation within an existing building in order to plan a route of access.

THE DISABILITY DISCRIMINATION ACT

The Disability Discrimination Act of 1995 has changed the legal obligations for historic properties in the UK. Its passage has not diminished the legal protections contained in existing conservation legislation, since the new Act does not override existing conservation legislation. It is still essential that any proposal to alter or demolish any part of a listed or scheduled structure or

2.2 Henry Moore Sculpture Gallery, Leeds.

The conversion and re-use of a nineteenth century Victorian terrace in Leeds provides a side access route for the Henry Moore Sculpture Gallery and Institute via a platform lift. Although this maintains the architectural integrity of the new main façade along Head Row the solution segregates disabled visitors from the main entrance.

one within a conservation area meet with the approval of the relevant conservation authorities.

The change in legal obligations comes about because the new law applies to existing buildings, whereas previously, access requirements were part of building regulations. These had little or no impact on existing buildings (and often on new buildings) and were generally viewed as an add-on rather than an integral part of providing for building users (Figures 2.2 and 2.3).[1] Now both sets of legal requirements must be considered: compliance with legal accessibility requirements and compliance with conservation requirements. For a minority of historic properties, conservation considerations may make it impossible to comply with the access requirements at a specific site, if they could harm or destroy the special architectural or historic interest. For the majority of sites, it is possible to devise an access strategy which meets both objectives.

The Act established the National Disability Council and the Northern Ireland Disability Council as independent advisory bodies to the government. The Councils will prepare codes of practice which will provide detailed guidance on the implementation of the Act. Shortly after the Act became law, the Minister for Disabled People issued a general summary of who will be affected by the Act. This brief guide to the Disability Discrimination Act provides the first official interpretation on the Act:[2]

Disabled people

The Act gives new rights to people who have or have had a disability which makes it difficult for them to carry out normal day to day activities. The disability could be physical, sensory, or mental. It must also be substantial and have a long-term effect (that means the disability must last or be expected to last for 12 months). Conditions

(a) (b)

2.3 Makin-Robinson Library, Downing College, Cambridge.

2.3 (a) Front elevation.

2.3 (b) Detail showing ramp to the side of the portico. John Preston, Conservation and Design Officer for Cambridge City Council explained the issue of access to the library in the following way: '[...] A major new classical building, entered through an imposing Doric portico off the main east–west axis leading from the porter's lodge into the College. Access was originally proposed via a ramp leading up to the side of the main entrance portico. The ramp would have been reached via a path leading from the drive into the College, but facing away from the rest of the College. In the course of negotiations, the architect was encouraged to set the building back on the site, and to consider providing a ramp leading to the centre of the portico; the ramp to the portico of the Temple of Apollo at Delphi was cited as a possible precedent (although much steeper). This suggestion did not find favour, and the architect proposed instead to relocate the access to the rear of the building which was not acceptable to the City Council. A compromise solution to the main entrance was agreed. The final result is asymmetric, with a ramp similar to that originally proposed but facing into rather than away from the College.'

which have a slight effect on day-to-day activities, but are expected to become substantial are covered. Severe disfigurement is also classified as a disability.

Employers and service providers

Employers and people who provide goods and services to the public will have to take reasonable measures to make sure that they are not discriminating against disabled people. Some people will have to take measures both as an employer and as someone who provides goods and services to the public.

Landlords and others who are responsible for letting or selling property

People who sell or let property will have to ensure that they do not unreasonably discriminate against people.

Prior to the adoption of the Disability Discrimination Act of 1995, there were two earlier forms of access legislation: national acts and the Building Regulations. The first act was known as the Chronically Sick and Disabled Act of 1970; it was amended in 1981 by the Disabled Person's Act. The access provisions relating to buildings and the environment were enacted but were never properly enforceable and then superseded by the regulations to the 1984 Building Act.

Definition of disability

Under the Act, disability is defined as a physical or mental impairment which has a substantial and long-term adverse effect on the ability to carry out normal day-to-day activities. This will include impairment to vision and hearing. Most disabled people will be covered by the definition although there will be some exceptions. The Secretary of State for Social Security may also issue guidance to assist in understanding and defining the terms.

This definition is fuller than the one provided by the Building Regulations which considered disability narrowly to be (a) an impairment which limits the ability to walk or which requires the use of a wheelchair for mobility; or (b) impaired hearing or sight.

In 1981 the World Health Organization produced an International Classification of Impairments, Disabilities and Handicaps. Impairment is 'any loss or abnormality of psychological, physiological or anatomical structure or function.' Disability is 'any restriction or lack (resulting from an impairment) of ability to perform an activity in the manner or within the range considered normal for a human being.' Handicap is 'a disadvantage for a given individual, resulting in terminology in legislation, administration, academic research and everyday speech, where the same terms are used for different concepts and different terms refer to identical concepts, causing confusion.' Another way of understanding 'handicap' is that 'a physical disability is only a handicap where it constitutes a barrier to the achievement of specific goals' and that people with disabilities are handicapped by buildings.

For buildings and sites the main provisions in the Act are contained in Part II, which applies to employees, and Part III which applies to members of the public.

Employment provisions

Part II requires employers to make reasonable adjustments for disabled employees to avoid 'substantial disadvantage'. There is an exemption for partnerships and small businesses under 20 employees.

This can apply to the physical features of a building or site. There may be a duty, given the facts and circumstances of each case, to make changes to the features of a building which affect a disabled person's ability to secure employment, including attending the pre-employment interview, or to engage in employment, opportunities for advancement, transfer, training or other benefits. Some of the examples of steps which affect buildings which may have to be taken, include:

- making adjustment to premises used for employment;
- assigning the disabled person to a different place of work;
- acquiring or modifying equipment.

What is reasonable?

In determining whether it is reasonable for an employer to have to take a particular step, factors such as financial and other costs to be incurred by the employer have to be taken into account. The extent of an employer's financial resources will be considered, as well as the availability of financial assistance from other sources.

It is not possible to state precisely what adjustments have to be made and when, since employees will be treated on a case-by-case basis.

Goods, services and facilities

Part III applies to a provider of goods, services or facilities which are normally provided to members of the public. The list of providers covered by the Act is broad and intended to be comprehensive. It covers access to and the use of any place to which members of the public are admitted. It covers facilities for entertainment and recreation, the services provided by any profession or trade and services provided by local or other public authorities.

What is required

The Act will require changes to the way goods, facilities and services are provided. It will be against the law for someone to run a service, or provide goods or facilities in a way which makes it impossible or unreasonably difficult for a disabled person to use the service or goods.

This can include the physical features of a building. For example, if the design or construction of a building or the approach or access to premises, makes it impossible or unreasonably difficult for disabled persons to make use of such a service, then the provider must take reasonable steps under the circumstances to remove the feature, alter it, provide a reasonable means of avoiding it or an alternative method of making the service available. The Act covers the use of aids and facilities to remove communication barriers for people with hearing and vision impairments.

Selling or letting land or property

People selling or renting property do not have to make adjustments to the property to make it accessible, but it will be against the law to discriminate against disabled people by, for example, charging a higher rent.

IDENTIFICATION AND ASSESSMENT OF PHYSICAL BARRIERS

In the historic environment, an audit of the existing physical features of a building or site to identify barriers is a two-step process. First the features which are barriers must be identified, then they must be assessed, individually and together. The assessment is the key determination and a far more sophisticated process. The goal of assessment is to determine if the features which are barriers are contributing factors to the special architectural or historic interest and whether there is an opportunity for alteration or change.

The conservation assessment will form part of the determination of when it is reasonable to take steps to meet the accessibility requirements under the Disability Discrimination Act (see note 10, Chapter 1).

2.4 Royal Academy, Burlington House, London.

Temporary ramp.

(*See page 26.*)

The need for listed building consent may often lead to the use of a temporary ramp or alternative door arrangement while a permanent solution is worked out, with temporary ramps a reminder of the continuing debate (Figures 2.4 and 2.5).

'In Norwich there is a ramp into the Tourist Office ... The rather tatty temporary ramp is there as a reminder of the continuing debate between city planners and English Heritage over what sort of access might be appropriate. They have gone through steel and stone and concrete and glass and the same old ramp is still here.' (Stephen Thorpe, Threshold Architects, Ipswich)

Conservation assessment

In the historic environment the basic presumption is against change. What are known as barriers in the access world may be important architectural features of the setting, like cobbled paths or courtyards, the architecture of the building, front entrance steps or a narrow doorway. Even details of original door hardware may be features which contribute to the special architectural or historic interest and so must remain unaltered and unaffected by access schemes.

In the general sense, an alteration is the destruction and/or removal of historic fabric or additions. This definition emphasizes retention of original and historical elements and embraces the concept that any alteration should be reversible. Individually and cumulatively, alterations and demolitions should not have an adverse affect on the building's special architectural or historic interest.

Within any historic building or site there will be features which contribute significantly to the special architectural or historic interest of the place. In the case of listed buildings, list descriptions seek to identify these principal features, but do not attach relative importance to them or aim to deal with them exhaustively. Generally, the principal elevations of a building, and its principal compartments and circulation areas, which will contain the principal staircase will be particularly important features contributing to its special interest.

2.5 Norwich Tourist Centre.

Temporary ramp.

How do these principles apply to the evaluation of access alterations? In the general sense, conservation authorities look most favourably on proposals which have the minimum physical effect on historic fabric, as well as the least visual impact. In addition to minimum intervention, proposals which avoid significant change to the principal features are likely to be more readily acceptable. In all cases the first step to planning an access strategy is to consider if there are ways to avoid the physical barriers through reversible alteration or finding new routes. Finding an alternative means of delivering the service is one of the stated methods of compliance with the Disability Discrimination Act. The alternative must be reasonable and not tantamount to discriminatory treatment.

These are some of the basic conservation factors which will affect the planning of an access strategy:

- extent of potential loss of the structure or the fabric of historic or architectural interest;
- degree of potential impact on the existing structure or the fabric of architectural interest;
- degree of potential impact on spatial qualities;
- degree of potential impact on architectural integrity;
- degree of potential impact on the interpretive role of existing structure or fabric;
- potential to alleviate wear on existing structure or fabric;
- potential level of capital costs;
- potential costs or loss of revenue associated with disruptions resulting from installation and closed periods;
- associated practicalities of increasing access;
- future work, including what the implications would be of seeking to secure access to the whole building. Although an installation of a front entrance ramp may be provided within one financial year, there may be plans in successive years to achieve access to first and other floors.

Assessment is done on a case-by-case basis, and what may be appropriate for one building or site may not be appropriate for another.

According to one English Heritage Historic Buildings Adviser, the criteria for assessment fall into five areas:

1. **The quality of the building and architectural elements, which includes the following considerations:**
   - **importance of the building;**
   - **location of the proposed access work;**
   - **sensitivity of the historic fabric.**

2. **Motivation for, alternatives to and scope of the proposals which includes the following considerations:**
   - **legal requirements;**
   - **political/public influences;**
   - **existing level of access provision;**
   - **intensification of use;**
   - **future phased works;**
   - **the permanence/reversibility;**
   - **alternative solutions.**

3. **Types of proposals for improving access:**
   - **ramps;**
   - **stairlifts and platform lifts;**
   - **passenger lifts and hoists;**
   - **automation of doors;**
   - **widening of existing openings;**
   - **handrails.**

4. **Quality of the design solution.**

5. **Effects on archaeology and hidden fabric such as floor beams and ceiling timbers.**[3]

Prioritizing access improvements

Many case studies reveal a pattern of establishing a priority for access improvements which can then be implemented over time. Full access should be viewed as a long term objective which will improve as the building goes through cycles of use and change. Improved access may not come about until a need for alteration comes about. Neither should opportunities be

2.6 Architectural Association, London.

Portable ramp.

missed. This is the role of the action plan (see inset on p. 21), to programme works and to use the opportunity of periodic maintenance to make improvements.

Administrative solutions

At some buildings or sites, administrative change may be a feasible alternative to physical intervention if the building owner can relocate its services and programmes to any accessible building, or an accessible part within a building, rather than modify an existing or historic building. Modifying the delivery of the service is another form of administrative solution.

Alternatives may include identification of the availability of services at other branches of the same business and can be a factor influencing the judgment on the need for proposals at a sensitive location. This point was discussed by the inspector during the public inquiry in Norwich (see Chapter One).

The concept of administrative solutions is embraced both in the Disability Discrimination Act and in heritage guidance. Planning and Policy Guidance Note 15, section 3.28 provides this suggestion: 'Alternative routes or re-organizing the use of spaces may achieve the desired result without the need for damaging alterations'.

The English Heritage Guidance Note, *Easy Access to Historic Properties*, makes the same suggestion (Figure 2.1).

> **Temporary solutions are generally only acceptable as interim measures while long-term solutions are worked out or where a permanent alteration would result in adverse impact. When it is necessary to use a temporary ramp, it may be preferable to use a portable ramp which is erected when the need arises and *removed* when not in use (Figure 2.6). This will avoid the visual clutter that temporary ramps add to historic settings but may not communicate to disabled people an affirmative access policy when only the barriers are visible (Figure 2.7).**

(a)

(b)

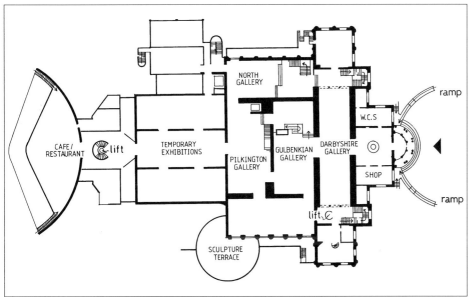

(c)

2.7 Whitworth Art Gallery, University of Manchester.

2.7 (a) Front elevation. The presence of a temporary ramp has helped the Museum establish strong links with disabled people while making permanent access improvements. Access works began in 1981 at the Gallery with the utilitarian temporary ramp, as shown in 2.7 (b). The gallery is committed to the use of a temporary ramp until the new permanent scheme, shown in 2.7 (c), is funded and built. English Heritage guidance acknowledges the need for managed ramps, ones which are constructed and removed. There is no clear guidance as to when a temporary ramp may be installed on a long term basis as a substitute for a permanent solution.

2.7 (b) Temporary ramp.

2.7 (c) The new scheme provides semi-circular ramps to the front façade which repeats the circular element of the curved portico to create an independent and permanent access solution to the front elevation of the Grade II* listed building.

In a recent report on proposed access improvements for the Palace of Westminster, an English Heritage inspector urged the Parliamentary Works Office to consider changes in administrative procedures for visitors and Members which would minimize the need for structural alteration to the Palace. The report further urged administrative change for disabled visitor access to St Stephen's Chapel through opening up a disused side entrance behind the altar. Otherwise access to the Chapel for wheelchair users would have been through the use of a platform lift fitted to the Chapel's early staircase.

In a similar context at the Dahl, the Irish Parliament Building in Dublin (Figure 2.8), Deputy Members literally vote by foot, walking up several steps towards the back of the House where Members assemble according to their position on matters of record. In this context, full participation would require far more extensive alteration than merely making the House accessible, since movement up the steps is part of the culture of the institution. While electronic voting would solve this problem, the change would alter the nature of the organization and may not be an appropriate administrative solution in this case. But this type of solution should at least be considered along with architectural solutions, even if ultimately rejected.

2.8 Linster House, Dublin, seat of the Dahl.

Middle Temple, London

Provision of an accessible public lavatory and conference facilities where barristers could meet their clients who cannot negotiate steps led the estates' department at Middle Temple, City of London to develop an accessible communal facility. The existing age, architectural and historic interest, and restricted space of individual chambers made common facilities an obvious solution rather than altering several chambers' entrances (Figure 2.9). Rooms within a lower ground floor were set aside for the meeting rooms and lavatories. Although the only available location was a lower ground level room, and access is via a platform lift device – a situation no one was happy with – the plan is one example of an administrative solution which has relieved the need for potentially more extensive and harmful alterations elsewhere within the individual chambers (Figures 2.9(b) and (c)).

Accessibility guidance and criteria

In recent years there has been an explosion in standards and design criteria. The Department of the Environment gives guidance in Part M and the Scottish Office provides guidance in Part T of the Building Regulations. The following is a list of official guidance.

British Standards

The British Standards Institute has issued a series of voluntary guidelines, including:

BS 5810 British Standard Code of Practice for Access for the Disabled to Buildings (1979)

BS 5619 British Standard Code of Practice for Design of Housing for the Convenience of Disabled (1978)

BS 5776 Specification for Powered Stairlifts (1979)

BS 6440 A Code of Practice for Powered Lifting Platforms for Disabled Persons (1983)

The role of the local authority access officer – Julie Fleck, Access Officer, Corporation of London

The post of access officer was first recommended in 1979 by government committee to establish a liaison point within local authorities on issues relating to the interests of disabled people. The first access officer was appointed by Leicester City Council in 1981 and there is now a national association. Most jobs are located either in the planning department or building control department, and occasionally within the social services, architects and engineers.

The aim of all access officers is to promote improvements in the built environment for disabled people.

The major tasks of the access officer include:

- **developing council policy on improving access;**
- **establishing procedures for implementing the policy;**
- **providing advice and guidance to local authority officers and others on the technical requirements;**
- **initiating a rolling programme of improvements;**
- **increasing the awareness of the access needs of disabled people;**
- **administering grants for improvements to premises;**
- **consulting and liaising with the local access group.**

On a day-to-day basis one of the most important areas of my work is examining planning applications. Major office redevelopment schemes, extensions, changes of use, even new shop fronts and minor alterations are examined. I negotiate with the applicant to ensure that access is considered at this early stage. It is much easier to redesign a ramp to reduce its gradient or to alter the layout of a WC while still on the drawing board than to wait until it is installed to tell the builder that the ramp is too steep, the WC cubicle is too narrow or the door opens the wrong way.

I also liaise very closely with the access group who help with surveys of buildings and streets and who discuss their access needs directly with designers. This helps to develop productive working relationships between planning applicants and local disabled people. This can form a greater understanding of access issues and usually produces a built environment more convenient and user-friendly for all of us.

BS 6083 British Standard for Magnetic Field Strength in Audio-frequency Induction Loops for Hearing-aid Purposes Part 4 (1991)

2.9 Middle Temple, London.

2.9 (a) Typical chambers entrance of narrow doorway and steep winding staircase.

2.9 (b) and (c) The original double-leaf entrance door was too narrow (less than 800 mm) for easy access for a wheelchair. The solution adopted retains the original doors which are joined to create a single leaf.

2.9 (d) The existing wooden balustrade leading from the entrance level to the lower ground floor ended in a quarter turn which made fitting a platform lift more difficult. Alterations to accommodate the platform lift eliminate the quarter turn to allow the platform lift to travel in a straight direction.

(*See page* 31.)

(a)

(b)

(c)

(d)

EU *guidance*

In 1972, the Council of Europe signed a resolution with a view toward making buildings more accessible for disabled people. In October 1987, the EU sponsored a conference in Utrecht on the accessibility of public buildings. The objective was to improve the accessibility of the built environment throughout the EU member states. In 1990, a Committee published the *European Manual for an Accessible Built Environment*. The 1996 final document is entitled *European Concept for Accessibility*.[4]

Fire safety

Building Regulations like Part M and Part T do not contain requirements relating to fire safety. This guidance is found separately in BS 5588 (Part 8), British Standard Code of Practice for Means of Escape for Disabled People (1988).

Urban design

Separate urban design laws were developed to guide the design of spaces between buildings, but do not contain specific regulations on the design aspects of the pedestrian environment for disabled people. One helpful publication is the Institution of Highways and Transportation guidelines, *Reducing Mobility Handicaps*. This document gives guidance on movement around the pedestrian environment, including aspects of the design of pavements, ramps, street furniture, the guarding of obstructions, crossing facilities and parking.

What are access needs?

The limited opportunity to make physical alterations makes it especially important to understand and assess exactly what the users' access needs are or will be. This approach brings a level of flexibility when devising an access strategy for historic building, since differing degrees and levels of access may be appropriate. All of the various standards and advisory guidance define access needs in terms of minimum dimensions for things like doors and slopes of ramps. The first step in identifying access needs is to understand what the users are doing at a particular building or site.

In a general sense, building users can be viewed as either *routine* or *occasional*. There will normally be both types of user. The type, location and administration of access like ramps, platform lifts, automatic doors and emergency evacuation depends largely on the building and whether the user is routine or occasional. The degree of staffing can also be an issue.

Routine users

Routine users are specific individuals who, on a daily or less frequent basis, visit the building or site and become familiar with its plan and circulation routes. Typical routine users may work within the building or site or visit it on a regular basis as part of carrying out official or work-related duties.

Occasional users

Occasional users are those in the population generally, of whom there can also be many or a few, who only make the occasional trip to the building or site and who thus do not become familiar with the building or site plan and its circulation arrangements. The number of occasional users will vary depending on the building function. A cultural monument may receive only one or two wheelchair users or blind visitors a week but provide for many older visitors, parents with young children and people with sight or hearing impairments.

The short circulation assessment

Audit checklists provide a detailed aid in assessment of physical and communication barriers. Design manuals give detailed information on accessible design criteria, largely based on the guidance set out in the Building Regulations and British Standards.[5]

It is easy to get bogged down using these long checklists when gathering information for the access strategy for a specific historic building or site. What is needed is a simple list of the minimum criteria which can be used to evaluate the extent of the circulation barriers so an overall strategy can be developed. The local access group can help by participating in the initial assessment. After the strategy is proposed the detailed assessment can come into play.

The following box provides a short checklist of the minimum criteria for wheelchair users and others using mobility aids to get in and around a building, use the toilets and get out in an emergency. It is intended to be used as an initial assessment of the major circulation barriers as part of the access assessment process. The criteria is the minimum widths and dimensions to evaluate existing features and does not always meet the recommendations of the Building Regulations. The Appendix contains a more detailed version for planning the fit out.

A short checklist for wheelchair access to existing buildings. More detailed criteria can be found in the Appendix

■ **Wheelchair size and clearances required**

Make provision for the larger models of electrically powered wheelchairs whose overall dimensions are approximately 675 mm in width and 1150 mm in length, you will then be assured of accommodating the small chairs, but these chair dimensions do not take account of the space needed to self-propel and to keep clothing and limbs free.

■ **Ramps**

Slopes

1:12 is the maximum slope permitted for a comfortable ramp for a wheelchair user or for an ambulant disabled person. There will be occasions where 1:12 is not possible, which would require careful consideration of the use and safety to design a steeper ramp.
1:15 is adequate.
1:20 is considered level.

Width

A minimum clear unobstructed ramp width of 900 mm; Part M recommends 1 m and a surface width of 1.2 m (including kerb).

Landings

Length 1.2 m, measured clear of any door swing.
Distance between landings depends on the ramp slope.
For slopes of 1:12 to 1:15, landings should be provided every 5 m.
For slopes of 1:15 to 1:20, landings should be provided every 10 m.

Handrails

For ramps over 2 m, there should be a continuous handrail on each side unless the ramps are symmetrical and there is a choice of handrails (Figure 3.7).

■ **Turning radius**

90° turn: as part of a circulation route on a ramp or in a corridor, a wheelchair can make a 90° turn if there is clearance of 900 mm width. Larger chairs can require a corridor space of 1400 mm by 1400 mm.
180° turn: for manual chairs the minimum clear space required is 1400mm by 1800mm. Larger chairs can require more space.

■ **Doors and lobbies**

External doors: minimum clear width is 800 mm.
Internal doors: minimum clear width is 750 mm.

Clear space from door edge: minimum width is 300 mm.

■ **Interior corridors**

Minimum clear width is 800 mm.
The preferred minimum for comfortable circulation is 1200 mm.

■ **Lifts**

Car size

Recommended minimum: 1100 mm wide by 1400 mm long.
Smaller existing lifts; access may still be possible depending on the individual orientation, as with through lifts.

Landings

1500 mm x 1500 mm in front of the door, can be smaller depending on approach.

Door

800 mm clear width.

■ **WCs**

Minimum room sizes

Wheelchair accessible: 1500 mm by 2000 mm.
Preferred minimum size: 2000 mm by 2500 mm.
Ambulant accessible: 800 mm by 1500 mm.

Door width and swing

800 mm clear width and opening outwards.

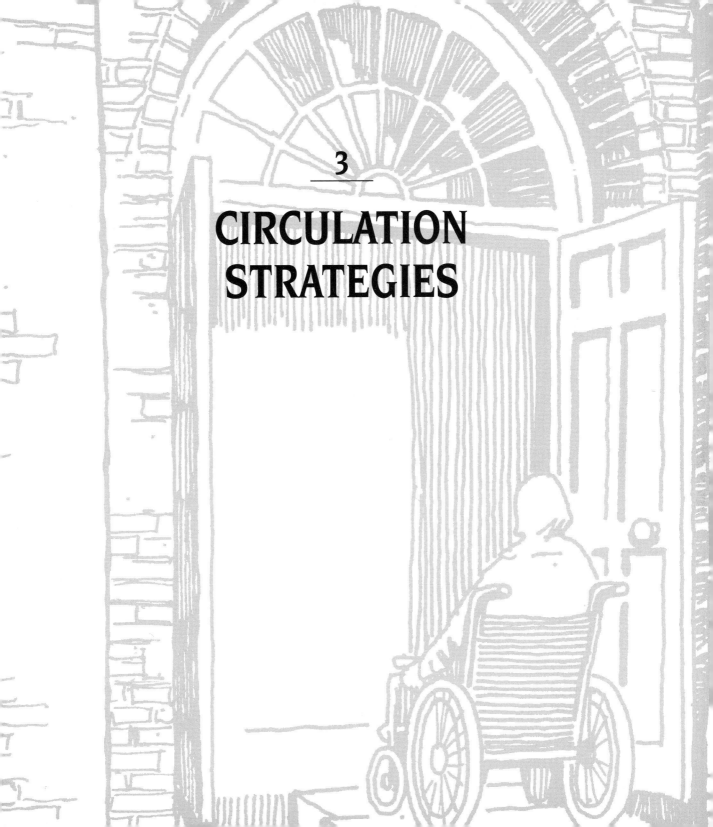

3

CIRCULATION STRATEGIES

The access assessment provides basic information which can be used to plan a route of access for wheelchair users and others who cannot negotiate steps. The starting point is to assess the options for getting into a building.

CHOOSING THE RIGHT ENTRANCE

In selecting the right entrance for an access route, the main elevation of a building may or may not have some flexibility for adaptation. With the social pressure to find front door solutions, knowing when a side door route makes sense and how to integrate separate entrances into the overall circulation planning can enhance the success of a scheme. The opportunity or

APPROACH FACTORS

Factors which influence where to provide a point of entry may include:

- place of arrival and mode;
- features of the layout or materials of the setting and approach to the building entrance;
- entrance features, including change of level;
- availability of space in front of the building;
- location of principal functions;
- internal features of the layout such as mezzanine level changes;
- circulation routes to lifts and accessible WCs;
- the ability to relocate functions.

APPROACH CHECKLIST

The checklist for evaluating the approach to a building or structure includes these items:

- proximity to parking or drop-off points or public transportation;
- gradient of slope and width of footpath;
- kerb drops;
- surfacing materials;
- lighting;
- signage.

limitation in choosing a point of entry will be the existing features of architectural interest on the approach to main internal circulation areas. The setting of the building, proximity to parking, drop-off points and surfacing materials found in historic environments can influence the choice of entrance. Internal layout can inspire or frustrate a strategy.

Once the overall circulation strategy has been defined it is then possible to focus on the related topics such as how to design external ramps and handrails for important elevations (Chapter Four); and when to use mechanical lift devices internally and externally for level changes where the space will not permit a ramp (Chapter Five). Case studies for these chapters are drawn from working buildings where there is scope for permanent or reversible alterations.

Many of the solutions illustrated in these chapters would be inappropriate, or indeed unnecessary, if the cultural significance of the building was as a place for interpretation or low economic use (as with places which are cultural monuments) as discussed in Chapter One. Circulation solutions to these building types are considered separately in Chapter Six where the schemes reveal a pattern of far less physical intervention and greater compromise on the degree of access independence and integration. The objectives are the same; there are just more compromises. For these types of buildings and structures, the access strategy may be more circumspect because of the architectural or historic importance of the building or site, and rely upon temporary measures and staff assistance to minimize physical alteration. The nature of the use gives more opportunity for emphasis on interpretation to supplement physical access.

For all buildings and sites, reconciling circulation planning with the potential impact of alterations on historic fabric, spatial qualities and architectural integrity is the essence of the problem in choosing the right entrance. One English Heritage Historic Buildings Adviser has summed it up this way:

> The type of structure will dictate the approach to a large extent. Thus a building which is architecture as architecture, the result of a considered design, will suggest an

approach which seeks to preserve that special design. A building which has developed as an organic structure may be important not for its authentic design, but for the survival of ancient fabric. This will dictate another approach, where visual considerations may be less important than the preservation of the fabric.[1]

Case studies and illustrations in this chapter are organized into groups of typical problems and solutions associated with choosing the right entrance. These studies illustrate where the access strategy has managed a successful balance between access and conservation considerations with minimum impact on original fabric and significant features, through a variety of design techniques.

Parking

Designated parking and set-down points should be provided and clearly signposted. The width of the standard parking bay needs to be increased by 1 m to allow for a transfer zone adjacent to the car for transfer as a passenger or driver. The route from the parking or drop-off point to the building or site entrance should be clearly marked.

Surfaces

Many historic buildings or structures are in settings with original historic features such as cobbles or setts. Conservation area and townscape schemes may have enhanced the historic character of the setting through the uses of traditional paving and surfacing materials (Figure 3.1). There are a variety of ways to alter the surfaces around buildings to provide a stable, firm route and tactile surfaces while retaining the historic character of the setting (Figure 3.2).

Signage

Good signage benefits all visitors and users. Signs should direct

The potential to alter the front entrance is one of the inherent opportunities or limitations which affect overall planning of accessible circulation routes. Individual features of a building's entrance may make it more or less amenable to alteration. The enclosed portal of Manchester Town Hall (Figure 3.16), proved too sensitive to alter. The open *porte-cochère* of Rochdale Town Hall lends itself to alteration with minimal intervention (Figure 3.5)

3.1 *Chapter Street, behind* York Minster.

Cobbles and other traditional paving materials can prevent access to historic places. York stone paviors provide a suitable alternative and can be integrated into cobbles and setts.

a person who cannot negotiate steps to the accessible entry and help guide blind and visually impaired people. Conservation constraints can influence the design and placement of signs, so

(a)

(b)

3.2 (a) Ironbridge Gorge, Shropshire.

Tactile paving used at pedestrian road crossings does not have to be visually intrusive if the materials and colours are sympathetic to the environment.

3.2 (b) Middle Temple, London.

Traditional paving stones can be used for kerb cuts in keeping with the character of buildings and their settings. (*See page* 37.)

as to be appropriate to the setting of a building or structure of historic importance (Figures 3.3 and 3.4).

Planning circulation

Circulation planning can be approached in the following ways.

Adaptation at the front entrance

This usually involves some degree of physical alteration and reconfiguration of the existing principal front entrance to cope with existing steps, by adding a ramp or in some way adapting the existing landscape or space in front of the

(a)

(b)

3.3 (a) Manchester Town Hall.

Embossed bronze signs on the Manchester Town Hall extension direct visitors to the entrance ramp.

3.3 (b) War Memorial Opera House, San Francisco.

Where permanent fixings may be inappropriate, free-standing signs can be used such as the sign at the War Memorial Opera House, San Francisco.

building. Regrading paving or tarmac under a *porte-cochère* is one example of intervention into the space in front of the building. This and other examples are illustrated in this chapter and Chapter Four (Figures 3.5–3.7 and 4.1–4.5).

Creating a new public entrance

A new point of entry can become the public entrance for *all* building users. New entry points can be through an existing or new side or rear opening or through a new extension (Figures 3.8–3.14).

3.4

Signs acknowledge that many facilities such as lifts which benefit wheelchair users have universal use.

3.5 Rochdale Town Hall, Lancashire.

3.5 (*a*) Front elevation of the Town Hall shown in an original water-colour painted before the original tower was destroyed by fire.

3.5 (*b*) View of steps and handrails introduced between the arches to accommodate the raised level of paving under the porte-cochère.

3.5 (*c*) View through side of the porte-cochère showing the raised level of paving.

3.5 (*d*) Ground floor plan: to create a new corridor from the entrance hall to the lift, the existing narrow door was widened and fitted with an automatic opener; existing walls and fittings in a WC were removed.

3.5 (*e*) Plan and sections of alterations to raise the level of paving within the porte-cochère.

(*See page* 42.)

(*a*)

(*b*)

(*c*)

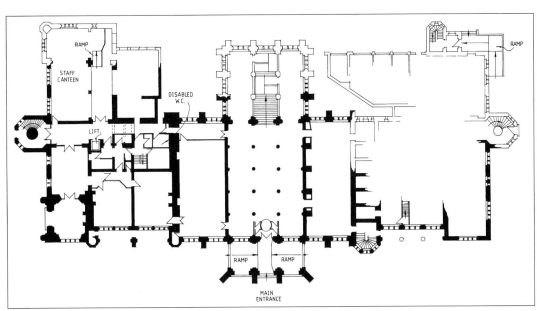

(d)

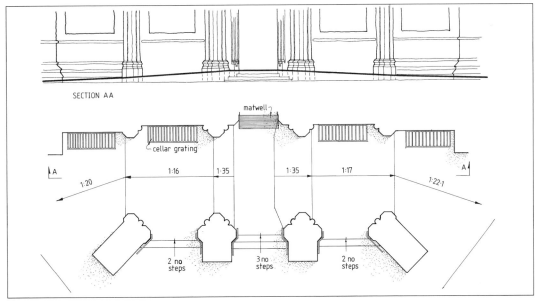

SECTION AA

matwell

cellar grating

1:20   1:16   1:35   1:35   1:17   1:22·1

2 no steps   3 no steps   2 no steps

(e)

Creating a separate point of level access

Not all buildings are capable of integrated adaptation to be usable by wheelchair users and others who cannot negotiate steps. A separate point of access may be necessary which links to internal circulation (Figures 3.15, 3.16 and 3.17).

FRONT ENTRANCE SOLUTIONS

Rochdale Town Hall

Rochdale Town Hall, Lancashire, is one of the dozen most ambitious High Victorian town halls of England (Figure 3.5). Described by Pevsner as 'picturesque', a centrally located Gothic Revival *porte-cochère* is one of the principal features of the Town Hall contributing to the building's special architectural and historic interest. Before adaptation, there were four steps at the threshold between the external ground level and the main ground floor within, leading to the vaulted hall, which was designed to be used as a wool exchange. Important principal rooms on the first floor included the Great Hall, a 90 foot long

ASSESSMENT OF CIRCULATION OPTIONS
An assessment of the existing architectural features revealed the building to be amenable to adaptation in a way which would not affect its special architectural or historic interest.

- **There was adequate space under the *porte-cochère* before the entrance.**
- **The change of level between external footway and entrance hall permitted a ramp of suitable grade, length and level.**
- **Internally, the existing level circulation on the ground floor could be adapted in a way which made a front entrance solution feasible.**
- **The existing screen with a central revolving door could be retained but adapted for wheelchair use – or so they thought (see top inset on p. 44).**
- **For vertical circulation to the upper floors, the existence of a service lift shaft could be expanded for use as a passenger lift, without undue structural alteration, or unacceptable loss of historic fabric or visual intrusion.**

room with a hammerbeam roof; the Mayor's suite; Council Chambers; and the Magistrates' Court. The main circulation route is via a great central staircase decorated with Gothic vaults and forming an imposing architectural feature of the entrance hall. An existing lift (see page 44 under Vertical circulation), added later, serves the upper floors but was not intended for general public use and was too small to accommodate a wheelchair. Nor was the lift location convenient for public circulation as it was situated in a corridor, well away from the main entrance hall and public circulation areas (Figure 3.5(d)).

Because of the civic nature of the functions contained within the Town Hall, the Council was concerned that the proposals should achieve an integrated and independent solution through the front entrance. In addressing this concern, Council architects had to consider whether there could be some alteration around the steps within the space of the *porte-cochère* and how to upgrade the lift for wheelchair use. Another barrier was the hand-carved screen with revolving doors inside the entrance foyer although this was not original to the building, but necessary to control the northern climate.

Entrance alterations

The basic concept of the scheme was to raise the level of the tarmac and stone paved areas adjacent to and under the *porte-cochère* by a total of approximately 500 mm to the top of the existing steps at the threshold. The design provides for the greater part of the existing steps to remain in place so the solution is reversible (Figure 3.5(e)). The outer edges of the ramp reach a near level gradient of 1:22; immediately under the arcade the slope increases to 1:17. Although recommended guidance suggests providing a handrail for any slope exceeding 1:20, the 1:17 gradient is gentle enough and does not pose a safety hazard thus avoiding the need for visually intrusive handrails (Figure 3.5(b) and (c) compared to Figure 3.6). Before the level entrance, the slope levels to a gradient of 1:35. These gradients generate a gentle sweep to the ramp, which does not add a visually intrusive diagonal element to the formal elevation.

To adjust for the effect of the raised paving, steps were introduced between the arches. Because of the slope away from the central bay, there are two steps in the side bays and three steps in the central bay. The steps help to re-establish the horizontal lines which are broken visually by the diagonal lines of the sloped tarmac ramp. Other case studies discussed later show that steps may be an appropriate design device to maintain the symmetrical and balanced composition of a classical façade when introducing the diagonal element inherent in an access ramp (Figures 3.9, 4.1, 4.4).

Because the scheme exploits the existing space and makes little change to the overall composition of the building, it has minimal impact on the character of the building. Where changes have been made – the steps introduced between the columns – these are conceived as a natural design device to cope with the level change.

Handrails

Handrails are fixed around the columns where the new steps have been introduced. The handrail design was developed from general historical precedent rather than from any existing design within the building. The handrail is constructed of wrought iron incorporating the Rose of Lancaster as an appropriate decorative motif. Another approach to handrail design is the duplication of the detail of existing railings, as was done for

3.6 Cheltenham Town Hall.

Front elevation; the new handrails along the slope of the ramp are incompatible with the existing mass of the carved stone balustrade, and tend to emphasize the alterations – an effect avoided in the scheme for the Rochdale Town Hall.

REVOLVING DOORS

Immediately inside the entrance foyer there was an existing screen with centre revolving doors and side swing doors. Rochdale Council experimented with fixing the existing revolving doors into an open position as part of the original access work so all visitors, including wheelchair users could use the same route – an important objective of the Council access policy. The alternative was to leave the revolving door functioning and have the existing side doors in the screen adapted for wheelchair use, but the Council viewed this as a segregated route for disabled people, and so unacceptable. After the first winter however, building engineers determined that the loss of the air-lock had caused an uncomfortable and unhealthy change in the ambient temperature of the lobby, resulting in higher than average staff illness. Following a change to the revolving doors at Manchester Central Library, similar problems were experienced when the revolving doors there were changed to permit wheelchair use. Rochdale Council decided they had to reinstate the revolving doors despite political sentiments. People who use wheelchairs accepted the compromise through the side doors, which were fitted with automatic openers.

Further controversy ensued however, over the wording for a sign to indicate the side door was independently accessible. Any reference to a 'disabled' entrance was rejected. The sign now reads 'automatic door', and is not labelled as a separate route for 'disabled people'.

the handrail added to the front elevation of Manchester Town Hall (Figure 3.16).

Vertical circulation

The existing passenger lift was upgraded to be wheelchair accessible for vertical circulation to the basement, first and second floors. Voice and tactile controls were added. As part of the upgrading scheme, the kitchen area was redesigned to create a new public corridor and lift lobby off the main entrance hall in order to avoid travel through adjoining committee rooms. This new route constitutes an obvious architectural change in order to enhance the utility of the existing lift for use by everyone including disabled people, and is the type of access

The existing passenger lift was constructed in 1905 with a brick rear half to the shaft and a full height timber front. The car, however, was too small to take a wheelchair. To minimize disruption to the fabric of the building it was decided that the rear part should be retained and the front extended in blockwork. This blockwork fulfilled two functions: first, support for the lift car guides, now further forward due to the larger car and revised winding gear position at the rear of the shaft; and second fire protection in line with other fire precaution work carried out two years previously. The new front was plastered with shoulder height panelling, cornice and door surround matching that to be found in the Town Hall. Blockwork was used to reduce weight, with the first and second floor sections being supported on new steel joists spanning the corridor at each floor level. The ground and basement sections were supported on a reinforced concrete suspended slab built into the basement walls, the weight of the ground floor section being transferred down through the brick arch at ground floor level. This slab was required due to the very poor ground conditions and a water table 1200 mm below the basement floor. The existing pit depth of 900 mm was maintained with special parts being manufactured by the lift supplier. The motor room is positioned in the basement. A new machine bed is being cast with special anchoring straps for the traction motor mounting steelwork to resist the upward loading. The top of the lift shaft is level with valley gutters on the roof. To relocate the motor room at the top of the shaft would have affected the roof line and was not acceptable for listed building consent.

Vincent Pool, Architect, Technical
Services Department, Rochdale Council

improvement that has universal benefit and creates an integrated circulation route.

Liverpool Town Hall

Liverpool Town Hall is an ornate late Georgian building built between 1749 and 1754 by the elder John Wood of Bath, with later additions by James Wyatt. Pevsner describes the whole as 'an exceptionally complete example of Late Georgian decoration and one of the best civic ensembles in the country' (Figure 3.7). Its famous dome was added later and dates from 1802. The portico to the principal entrance which was the focus of the access works was also added later, in 1811. It is enclosed on its sides and was originally approached with two steps rising approximately 350 mm from the external footway to the porch level.

Although the portico has enclosed sides, its generous internal proportions made it possible to plan alterations within its volume so as to minimize the visual impact of access ramps to the whole of the formal elevation. The scheme was designed by architects Donald W. Insall and Associates. From the footway, the scheme eliminates the steps between the centre arch by lowering the floor level and re-works the existing space under the portico into a pair of symmetrical dog-leg ramps, with a gradient of 1:16 (Figure 3.7(a)). The ramps are fitted with a continuous central wrought iron handrail.

(a)

(b)

3.7 Liverpool Town Hall.

3.7 (a) View within portico after alterations showing handrails and symmetrical dog-leg ramps.

3.7 (b) Interior view of council chamber showing ramped access over existing level change.

On axis with the entrance door in the centre bay are two new stone steps located within the portico at mid-point. They reinforce the original architectural approach to the entrance. These steps also offer an alternative to ramped access. The stone landing immediately before the door is ribbed as a tactile warning to visually impaired people to alert them to the centrally located steps, since additional handrails leading from the door to the pavement would interfere with access to the ramps.

Interior circulation

The principal circulation route through the ground floor is on the level until the Council Chamber, where there is an approximately 300 mm change of level leading into the Council Chamber from the main floor level. Symmetrical interior ramps were placed in the gallery area and are incorporated into the existing steps at the two chamber entrances (Figure 3.7(b)). The panelled sides to the ramps are based on existing decoration in the Chamber. New ramps replace steps where the floor level descends toward the podium.

Although interior changes were extensive to permit wheelchair users to get into the Chamber, access to the Members' setting could not be satisfactorily resolved. The existing Members' setting was fixed and removing sections to provide wheelchair spaces was considered too disruptive. Although an acceptable solution to the Members' setting was not part of the original works, the scheme shows how it is possible to make moderate circulation improvements without resolving all access issues.

CREATING A NEW PUBLIC ENTRANCE

Church House

Church House, Westminster, London, was designed by Sir Herbert Baker in the 1930s and serves as the home for the General Synod of the Church of England. Its main ceremonial entrance opens onto a large enclosed courtyard to the South of Westminster Abbey known as Dean's Yard (Figure 3.8(a)). The principal feature of the main entrance is its neo-classical portico which sits on an elevated plinth. The sides of the portico are enclosed. Although Dean's Yard affords space before the building, the porches' closed sides and steepness of rise of the porch limit the opportunity to exploit the porch in the same ways as either Rochdale or Liverpool were handled. The physical limitations at the front entrance were compounded by its generally inaccessible location for members of the general public, who tend to arrive at a side location along Great Smith Street because of its convenience to bus, taxi and other routes.

Although Dean's Yard remains the main ceremonial entrance, the entrance off Great Smith Street is more convenient for use by the general public, and is architecturally more amenable to alteration rising only three steps. Looking at the building and established public circulation flexibly and pragmatically, it made sense to treat the Great Smith Street as a new integrated public entrance which would also be accessible to wheelchair users and those who cannot negotiate steps (Figure 3.8(b)).

Inside the building there were several level changes along the principal circulation routes, including a mezzanine level and split levels on the first three floors. Existing lifts provide vertical access between floors leading to the Assembly Hall and the Hall of Convocation and other principal function areas, but level access to and from the lifts was hindered by the intermediate level changes.

This still necessitated several internal changes to overcome the diversity in levels. Internal circulation from the Great Smith Street entrance foyer originally led onto a short flight of three steps leading to the mezzanine level associated with the Dean's Yard entrance. Existing lifts provide access to the first floor level where a further five steps lead to the ambulatory corridor.

The internal spaces are composed of offices and a series of assembly halls and conference rooms. The principal space is the circular Assembly Hall, and main circulation routes are via the ambulatory.

Refurbishment and access alterations came about when the Corporation for Church House was considering ways to increase the commercial viability of the building through exploring the

(a)

(b)

3.8 Church House, Westminster.

3.8 (a) Dean's Yard entrance.

3.8 (b) Great Smith Street entrance after alteration.

3.8 (c) Interior view of lobby.

(c)

potential use of the building's halls and meeting rooms as separately marketable public facilities. When considering the proposed new use by church delegates and general public, the Corporation's management and architects defined their access objective:

> It was an aim shared by ourselves and the client that all delegates should be treated equally ... We did not want disabled visitors being told to enter by the garage entrance and make their way via a series of back corridors and office lifts to the same rooms that able-bodied visitors had reached without leaving the area occupied by the conference centre.
>
> Martin Fox, Lawray Architects, London

Alterations

The external alterations at the Great Smith Street entrance operate in tandem with interior circulation changes, to form an accessible route from Great Smith Street to the main function areas, toilets and the existing lifts.

The original flight of three steps, rising from the pavement in Great Smith Street to the enclosed entrance porch, were replaced with a ramp. The enclosed nature of the porch restricted the available space for the ramp so the resulting slope has a greater than desired gradient which means some wheelchair users may require assistance. To accommodate for the steeper than normal ramp, lobby staff have been trained to offer appropriate assistance. It is an important principle of any access work in public buildings that management and administrative measures may have to compensate where full compliance with the guidance – like that of slope gradients – is not possible because of existing restraints such as a narrow porch.

The ramp from the street entrance extends into the entrance foyer to reduce the overall gradient to 1:12. The ramp was formed in concrete with a finish to match the existing adjacent terrazzo flooring (Figures 3.8(c) and (d)).

To maintain the integrity of the Great Smith Street façade, the existing doors and iron gates had to be modified for re-use to compensate for the change in the porch floor level. The bottom rails of the existing doors were extended and the iron gates were re-hung onto a raised plinth to take account of the lowered level of the entrance porch.

In the entrance foyer, an existing staircase leads down to the basement floor. Earlier alterations had made the staircase redundant. The space over the staircase was of adequate width for a ramp adjacent to the existing steps leading to the mezzanine level (Figure 3.8(d)). The result is a discreet, continuous, albeit steeper than normal ramp, from the lower level Great Smith Street pavement to the mezzanine level inside the building.

On the first floor level, the five steps leading to the ambulatory were adjacent to an existing light well. Through earlier alterations, a portion of the light well had been infilled for lavatory and storage facilities. Through imaginative reconfiguring and extending the usable space in the light well it was possible to append an access ramp to the exterior of the building to provide level circulation from the first floor level to the second mezzanine level. Although the ramp departs from the normal

---

PASADENA CITY HALL, CALIFORNIA

An enclosed porch at the Pasadena City Hall in California presented design difficulties (Figure 3.9). The architects from Architectural Resources Group, San Francisco, studied various ramp and lift alternatives but concluded that neither approach would be appropriate because of the potential for significant adverse impact on the porch and front elevation. This assessment prompted a scheme to re-orient the main public entrance to the rear elevation, which was more amenable to alteration. The building was designed around a central courtyard and the rear elevation which had not been completed. A series of ramps and steps lead to a new arcade which completes the formal courtyard.

(a)

(b)

3.9 Pasadena City Hall, California.

3.9 (a) Front entrance portal.

3.9 (b) Aerial view of rear elevation: arcade completes rear elevation and provides new public entrance.

circulation route, it rejoins the general circulation route at the ambulatory level.

These alterations follow the advice of PPG 15 to use flexibility and imagination in planning accessible circulation routes.

CHANGE OF USE

A circulation strategy can evolve, responding to existing architectural limitations and opportunities, at alternative entrances when the building is undergoing a change of use.

St George's Hall

St George's Hall, Liverpool (Figure 3.10), was originally conceived as a concert hall, but when public subscriptions failed to raise the necessary funds, the City of Liverpool modified the brief to include assize courts within the building. The resulting building, based on plans by Harvey Lonsdale Elmes and finished by C. R. Cockerell, has been described as one of the finest neo-Grecian buildings in England and the world.

After court functions were shifted to a new, more modern

3.10 St George's Hall, Liverpool.

3.10 (a) Front elevation.

3.10 (b) Temporary ramp to front elevation.

3.10 (c) North entrance where ramped access is proposed.

3.10 (d) Plan for alterations to North entrance.

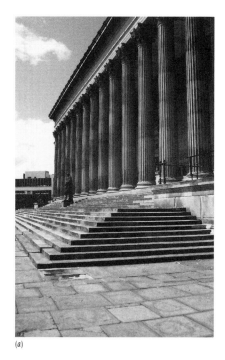

(a)

(b)

(c)

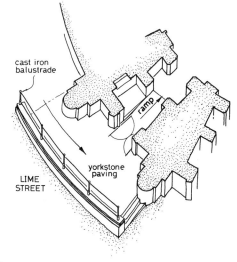

(d)

facility, the decline of Liverpool's economy and the cost of maintenance closed the concert hall temporarily in 1984. Through a city partnership funding scheme, Liverpool Council obtained initial funding for major repairs to meet current building regulations as the first phase of work bringing this important building back into use. In 1988, following this first phase refurbishment work the building was re-opened for limited public use. It was at this time that a temporary ramp to the east main entrance was erected to accommodate wheelchair visitors during a three week summer musical festival. This temporary ramp has remained in place as the Council works to raise the funds for the second phase of work which will include access improvements (Figure 3.10(b)).

The scheme by architects Buttress Fuller Geoffrey Allsop Practice provides for a new public entrance to be established to the north end. The intent is to shift permanently general circulation into the building from the main east entrance to the north entrance, which is more architecturally amenable to alteration (Figure 3.10(d)). The north entrance is approached through a few steps from the level of the pavement (Figure 3.10(c)). Access through the south portico and other routes was also studied, but rejected.

A new public entrance at the north elevation makes sense because of the existing physical opportunities at this location. Changing the circulation also works with the proposed new long-term use of the hall. Concert functions will return to the Concert Room at the north end and the Great Hall and related facilities will occupy the assize courts. The north entrance will become the principal entrance for proposed visitor facilities and concert performances. New lifts adjacent to a semi-circular ambulatory of the north entrance will provide vertical access.

Padiham Town Hall

Padiham Town Hall, Lancashire, features a stone portico to a 1938 brick building (Figure 3.11). When the town hall functions were merged with those of an adjacent borough, the Town Hall was made redundant. Three unrelated new uses now fill the building: a municipal library, offices for housing services and a social club. The distinct nature of the three new uses and alternate hours of public opening did not facilitate a central entrance or internal connections. Instead, a more *ad hoc* approach was taken with individual entrances created to each area of the building with the result that the original architectural entrance through the portico was no longer needed (Figure 3.11(b)). The entrance has been sealed, and access for the three uses occurs at the sides of the building. Access for disabled people thus required three separate external ramps. Figure 3.11(c) is a typical example of the simple style adopted for these side-location ramps. Although fortuitous, these separate access solutions avoid the need to alter the original architectural entrance which features steps rising from the pavement to a formal portico.

EXTENSIONS

A new entrance can be created when there is the opportunity of a planned extension of the existing facilities, as part of a change of use or a re-development of the current use. Whether an extension to an existing historic building is appropriate depends on its impact on the setting and existing features of architectural and historic interest. New extensions can minimize the alteration of existing external and internal features in the historic part of the building.

The Square Chapel

The Square Chapel, Halifax, is an eighteenth-century Grade II listed building, which occupies a prominent position, but the rear elevation connects more naturally to existing activities of the city centre and the adjacent Piece Hall (Figure 3.12). During the nineteenth century the building was used as a school. The building was derelict when acquired by a local building preservation trust for use by a charitable performing arts trust (Figure 3.12(b)).

3.11 Padiham Town Hall, Lancashire.

3.11 (*a*) Front elevation.

3.11 (*b*) Plan showing original layout of Town Hall and access ramps to side entrances.

3.11 (*c*) View of ramp to side elevation.

(*See page* 51.)

(*a*)

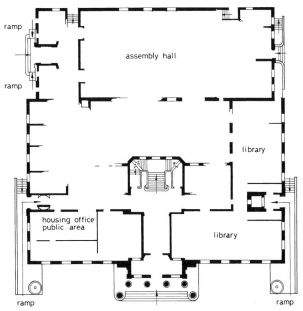

(*b*)

(*c*)

(a)

(b)

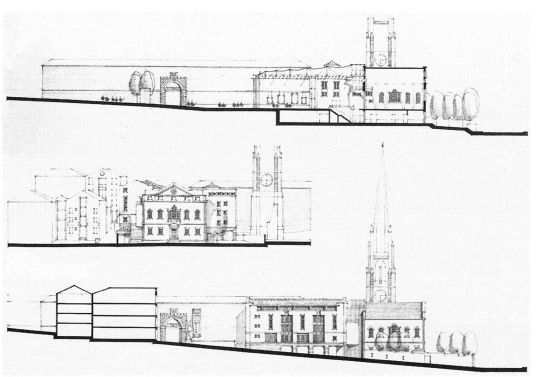

(c)

3.12 The Square Chapel, Halifax.

3.12 (a) Historical view of front elevation.

3.12 (b) Chapel in distressed condition.

3.12 (c) Section through the site development showing the south gate of Piece Hall over-looking new public space together with Square Chapel Performing Arts Centre; elevation of Square Chapel and Piece Hall and section looking towards Piece Hall and Square Chapel.

(*See page* 51.)

When the original trust architects began developing a conservation plan for the building, three key issues emerged which affected the planning of a circulation strategy:

- Evidence from historic photographs and survey work revealed the original configuration of the entrance steps which had been removed from the front elevation, an important architectural feature which could be restored with the evidence. To reinstate the steps would conflict with the objective to develop an accessible, integrated public entrance.
- A first floor had been inserted into the chapel during the nineteenth century when the building had been used as a school. Retaining the floor would provide the desired performance space and release the space at ground level for administrative offices and dressing rooms for performers. This created vertical circulation problems since the building was too small to admit a passenger lift.
- Another factor which influenced the planning of use was the desire to re-orient the public entrance to relate better to the activities at Piece Hall and the city centre to the rear of the site.

The original scheme by Allen Todd Architects, Leeds, balances all these objectives by developing a master plan for the site redevelopment. The scheme creates a new public entrance to the rear elevation, with extensions. Inherent site factors and the existing first floor in the Chapel inspired the scheme, which uses the natural slope across the site from the Piece Hall to the rear elevation. This allows for direct level circulation into the first floor performance area (Figure 3.12(c)). Reorienting the public entrance to the rear elevation made it feasible then to reinstate the front entrance steps without creating a segregated route of access for people who could not negotiate steps. Vertical circulation is provided in the extension.

Irish Linen Museum, Northern Ireland

The Irish Linen Museum, Lisburn, occupies the historic Lisburn Market House and Assembly Rooms buildings (Figure 3.13).

These buildings have a 300-year history and association with the political and social history of the city of Lisburn, a natural setting for a regional history museum. The existing buildings survive largely from the nineteenth century. Conversion of the use of the buildings began when the Market House arches were bricked up. An elaborate Italianate style scheme in 1889 added further architectural interest. The building passed through private ownership until Lisburn Urban District Council acquired the buildings in 1901. In 1981 the Lisburn Museum opened.

A 1992 extension scheme created a new exhibition space, an accessible entrance through a new foyer linking the extension to the Market House (Figure 3.13(a)). The extension accommodates a café, museum shop, offices on the upper floors and lift access to all upper areas, something not possible in the historic building. The new foyer space provides a level circulation link to the existing museum in the Market House. Visitors begin a sequence of ground floor exhibitions in the historic Market House. The existing change of level has been overcome with a gentle ramp which is integrated into the exhibition display raising the overall floor level of the display galleries. The visitor circulation route continues to the first floor via an historic staircase (Figure 3.13(b)). At first floor level the Assembly Rooms link to the extension and new exhibition galleries.

Visitors who cannot negotiate the steps between the ground floor and the first floor have to retrace their route through the entrance foyer, where they can use the lift in the extension to rejoin the circulation route in the first floor gallery.

Manchester City Art Gallery

The existing Manchester City Art Gallery was built as the Royal Manchester Institution by Sir Charles Barry between 1824 and 1835. It features a Grecian portico which leads into a fine entrance and staircase hall (Figure 3.14). The Gallery uses the former Athenaeum, also by Barry, as an annexe. Access into the Gallery and annexe is via one of two substantial flights of steps. When access to the principal entrance was considered, the only plausible solution was a long pair of ramps, each 44 m to the

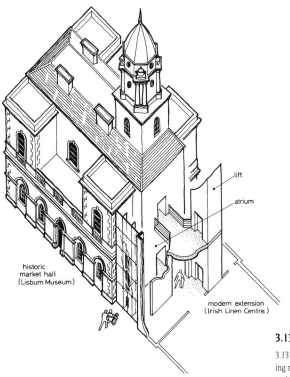

(a)

(b)

3.13 Irish Linen Museum, Lisburn, Northern Ireland.

3.13 (a) Illustration showing historic market house and glazed atrium linking modern extension. Early buildings were destroyed by fire during the
Irish Rebellion of 1641, and a later market house was destroyed, also by
fire, in 1707. Stonewall fragments and a sandstone arch in the entrance
hall remain and form the core of the existing buildings.

3.13 (b) Historic staircase within the market house: the original scheme
proposed a custom-designed lift to be inserted in the restricted space of
the stairwell so visitors who cannot negotiate steps can continue along the
principal circulation route within the market house to the first floor assembly rooms. The staircase is an important architectural feature, but conservation authorities had accepted the lift scheme. In its free-standing
position within the stairwell, the lift shaft does not require loss of historic
floor members, or damaging alterations to the staircase or balustrade. (See
discussion in Chapter 5, on conservation considerations when evaluating
the impact when planning lift additions.) After lengthy negotiations the lift
scheme was abandoned because the limited space of the stairwell resulted
in an internal car size less than that specified in British Standards. The
view shows how the floor level from the adjacent gallery into the stairwell
was raised to provide level access to the lift.

3.13 (c) Platform lift in new extension provides for change of site level.

(c)

3.14 Manchester City Art Gallery.

Front elevation.

(*See page* 54.)

As part of a feasibility study for the re-development of the site of the Manchester City Art Gallery, access objectives and conservation requirements were identified.

1. All visitors entering the buildings which make up the Manchester City Art Gallery, whether able-bodied or not, should use the same routes throughout.

2. The buildings should accommodate the needs of people with any kind of disability.

3. Where possible, full access should be achieved without disturbing the Grade I listed façade and interior of the Manchester City Art Gallery.

4. There should be WCs available for disabled people at all levels, open to the public.

5. There should be access for disabled staff to all offices and stores, with accessible toilet facilities on the office level. This would also open up these areas to disabled students, researchers and colleagues from other museums and galleries wishing to study items in store.

Excerpts from the feasibility study for the Art Gallery,
Master Plan for Access and Site Development.

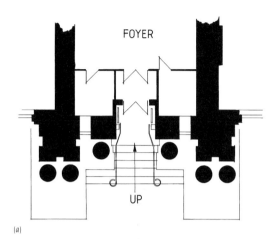

FOYER

UP

(a)

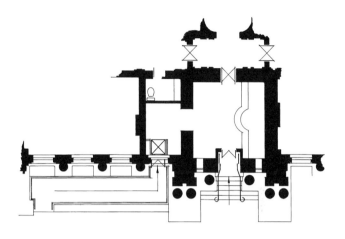

(b)

(c)

(d)

3.15 Municipal Buildings, Liverpool.

3.15 (*a*) Front entrance arrangement.

3.15 (*b*) Partial ground floor plan showing the proposed ramp over the basement area inside the existing stone balustrade at front elevation.

3.15 (*c*) Break in balustrade at front elevation.

3.15 (*d*) Ramp over the basement area from the level of the footway to the lower ground floor level lift.

(*See page* 58.)

existing entrance. This solution was considered poor value for money as it would have a major impact on the architectural features of the original entrance and would only provide access to the upper ground floor of the existing building while a majority of the Gallery's collection is housed on the first floor. Installing lift access from the ground floor to the first floor would not be possible without destroying both the symmetry of the internal layout and fabric of the Grade I listed building. The entrance to the Athenaeum did not offer further scope.

The Gallery has undertaken an extensive feasibility study as part of a major redevelopment scheme. Access plays a key in the development brief (see details on page 56). The feasibility study looked at ways to create an alternative main entrance with new reception facilities in a new extension building. The extension would also provide lift access to the basement and upper floors and the new buildings could be linked to the old through ramps and a bridge at upper levels.

COMPLEMENTARY ENTRANCES

If the nature of existing architectural features limit the opportunity for alteration and there is no opportunity to create a new public entrance through an existing side or rear elevation or through an extension, access can be provided through a side entrance away from the main circulation route. This may sometimes require creating a new opening into the building.

Municipal Buildings, Liverpool

The Municipal Buildings, Liverpool, dates from 1860 to 1866 and was designed by the Corporation Surveyor, John Weightman. The building serves important civic functions as an adjunct to the Town Hall. Architecturally, the building is large and symmetrical along the front elevation. The entrance is defined by the giant pilasters and attached columns which provided little opportunity for alteration (Figure 3.15). A new entry point is created at the lower ground floor level where a platform lift provides access to the general lobby area (Figure 3.15(b)). A

break in the original stone balustrade along the front elevation leads to a new ramp from the level of the footway over the basement area to the lower ground floor (Figures 3.15 (c) and (d)). These alterations only affected minor elements of the building and did not affect its special architectural or historic interest. The alternative point of entrance could be seen as a compromise from the user's point of view (being away from the main entrance). The proximity to the main entrance and limited scope for alteration there makes the compromise necessary in order to secure a workable solution which balances both conservation and access considerations.

Manchester Town Hall

Manchester Town Hall is considered one of the finest Victorian public buildings in England. It is an example of the symmetrical Victorian Gothic composition of Alfred Waterhouse and is Grade I listed, occupying a prominent position in Alfred Square (Figure 3.16). Below the centrally located tower is a large portal which serves as the main entry. The building is now linked to a 1938 extension on the adjacent street and visitors and staff routinely enter the building from the side door, and make use of a connecting overhead footbridge.

Although the building can be approached from other routes, the enclosed portal is undeniably the principal architectural feature of the building facing into Albert Square, and so the Council were interested in achieving an access solution through this principal entry. The enclosed portal rises up five steps from Albert Square.

From a conservation point of view, a front door solution was problematic from the start. The portal is such an important feature of the building's character. Its ornamental and enclosed design provided little scope to adapt the entrance with ramps to achieve level access, unlike the more generous entrances at Liverpool and Rochdale Town Halls, despite the same Council policies favouring front door solutions. The portal is also too narrow and too important to admit a mechanical device.

Even if the portal had been more amenable to alteration,

internal level changes in the entrance hall would have made a front door solution unworkable. The first entrance hall gives way to a second further elevated hall where the two principal staircases are located. A further three steps leads to the main hall (Figure 3.16(b)). The change in level between the entrance halls is an integral part of the interior architectural features; the use of two platform lifts for wheelchair users would have been too cumbersome and not useful to others not in wheelchairs but who cannot negotiate steps.

When viewed in a flexible and pragmatic way, a side door ramp on the extension side leading directly into the second entrance hall and main circulation areas made more sense than a series of potentially adverse alterations of limited use. It is closer to accessible parking bays and allows visitors to circulate

(a)

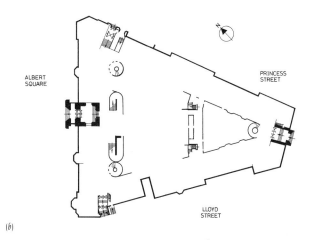

(b)

3.16 Manchester Town Hall.

3.16 (a) Front elevation.

3.16 (b) Ground floor plan.

3.16 (c) Side elevation showing view down the ramp. There has been controversy concerning the massive and enclosed nature of the stone ramp structure, and as to whether it is the right approach for both the users and the building.

(c)

between the lower floors of the Waterhouse building and the extension building (Figure 3.16(c)).

Museum of Farnham

Many domestic buildings find new uses. The small scale of these buildings and their architectural and historic interest can restrict and limit the opportunities for level routes of access through the original principal entrance, which in part explains the lack of examples of good solutions.

In some cases the building itself may be an important artefact of historical and social development. The architecture and its furnishings may be the principal reason for the visit as in the case of buildings associated with important social figures. The building may be otherwise a rare surviving building type. Other buildings are converted to museum use and the collections may be the principal reason for visiting the building.

The Willmer House, Farnham, is a Grade I listed early Georgian house dating from 1718 (Figure 3.17). The house is now used as the Museum of Farnham. It presents the typical access issues when small domestic buildings are converted to public uses – stepped access at the principal door leading to a delicate entrance hall and an important original staircase for access to the first floor (Figure 3.17(b)).

(a)

(b)

3.17 Museum of Farnham, Surrey.

3.17 (a) Front elevation: internal links from the entrance in the adjacent dwelling provides access to the Wilmer House.

3.17 (b) Detail of historic balustrade: rarely will it be appropriate to install a platform lift at the principal entrance or on an important historic staircase. Mechanical installations are more commonly located in side locations to avoid the visual impact on principal elevations and damage to the fabric of the original staircases. The alternative solution of placing a passenger lift within the building was considered too damaging. The result is that vertical circulation to the first floor is not possible for anyone who cannot negotiate steps.

Initial improvements in the 1980s provided for wheelchair access by a side door located through the garden wall, an entrance described by the curator as definitely feeling like a 'tradesman's' entrance.

When a structural survey revealed the need for conservation works, this provided an opportunity to create a new route of access for wheelchair users through an adjacent building with internal links to the museum. Although this is still a separate entrance for wheelchair users, it is considered an improvement over the back door scheme since access is at the front and the internal corridor joins directly into the main entrance hall and circulation route.

PORTABLE RAMPS

THE FAN MUSEUM

A solution of last resort, especially for small buildings with flexible staffing is to use a portable ramp. At the Fan Museum, Greenwich, London (Figure 3.18), the preferred option was to ramp over the front steps at the entrance, but conservation officials from the borough and English Heritage would not accept this alteration to the front entrance of this Grade II* listed Georgian terraced house, and there was no suitable side entrance. The Museum settled on the use of a portable ramp which consists of two folding metal tracks for wheelchair users. The suitability of this option takes account of the availability of discreet staffing. Other details of the building are discussed in Chapter Five.

3.18 Fan Museum, Greenwich, London.

Temporary ramp rails at front elevation of this typical eighteenth-century entrance in which the original door step and York paviors are important features contributing to the building's character. The door bell is not accessible from a wheelchair, so a visible and accessible call button before the entrance is advisable where assistance is required since visitors in wheelchairs may arrive independently.

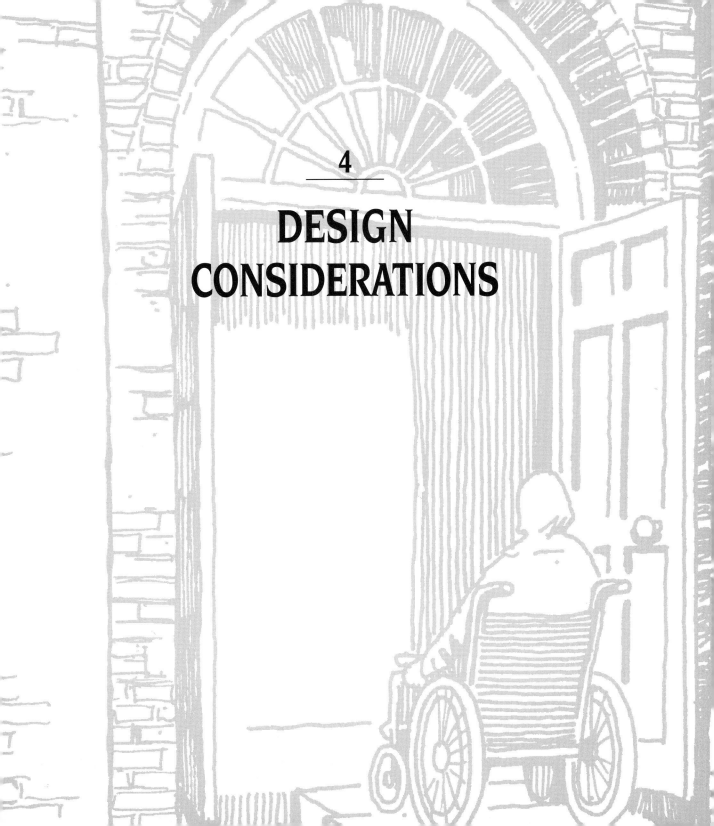

4

DESIGN
CONSIDERATIONS

Once lost, listed buildings cannot be replaced; and they can be robbed of their special interest as surely by unsuitable alteration as by outright demolition.[1]

The starting point for determining an application for consent for the alteration, extension or demolition of a listed building, is that there should be 'special regard to the desirability of preserving the building or its setting or any features of special architectural or historic interest which it possesses.' This permits authorities to control unnecessary demolition and unsuitable and insensitive alteration.[2]

Determining an application for the alteration, extension or demolition of a building within a conservation area is that 'special attention should be paid . . . to the desirability of preserving or enhancing the character or appearance of the area.'

ARCHITECTURAL VALUE

For a building of special architectural or historic interest, its design value can be as a surviving example of a particular architectural style or period of building, like the Georgian terraced house which is now the Museum of Farnham (Figure 3.17). The period or style within a period may also be associated with its author, as in the case of the symmetrical compositions like Manchester Town Hall which distinguished the High Victorian style of Alfred Waterhouse from that of his contemporaries (Figure 3.16), and the Greek Revival style of the Ashmolean Museum, Oxford, by C. R. Cockerell (Figure 4.2). The emphasis is on the visual aspects of original contributing elements and the aesthetics of the whole composition.

Professional, analytical and critical assessment can help to identify those intrinsic qualities which contribute to a building's design value. A resource may be compared to similar structures and sites to establish the relative significance to its own time, to other periods and to the present. Rare and unique resources typically are of greater value because fewer remain in existence, so less change is likely to be permitted.

AUTHENTICITY

The concept of 'authenticity' discussed in Chapter One in relation to the preservation of the physical materials of a historic building or structure also applies to the design features and composition as a whole. While 'authenticity' in materials is based on values found in the physical substance of the original heritage resource, authenticity in design is related to the architectural, artistic, engineering and functional design of the monuments, site or landscape, and the relevant setting. The authenticity of its design can either enhance or diminish the legibility of the original design intent. On a day-to-day basis the listed building and/or planning process controls any proposed external alteration to the fabric of a structure or changes to its appearance or setting. In practical terms this means that conservation control may be exercised in many areas over design aspects of alterations, affecting the choice of materials and methods of construction.

New elements like ramps and handrails must be designed in a way which also preserves a building or structure's architectural harmony. Technical, structural and functional concepts as well as craftsmanship and choice of materials can also contribute to architectural harmony and design and should be taken into consideration when designing alterations. As with repair work, the standard for new work is that it should be done without historic or artistic deception, and in a manner which maintains the quality of the original workmanship of original features.

The principles which come into play in design and evaluation of new elements can be summarized this way:

- New elements should not disrupt the authenticity of the existing structure.
- New elements should harmonize with existing features.
- New elements should integrate into the original design intention.
- Existing design language should be the inspiration and a source of moderation.
- New elements designed in a modern idiom may be

appropriate in some circumstances, where they meet the above criteria.

REVERSIBILITY

The reversibility of solutions needs to be considered. Conservation authorities will seek design solutions and construction methods which protect, preserve and maintain as much of the original fabric as possible, even where the principle of change is acceptable. However, 'Reversibility should not be used to justify solutions of an insensitive or inappropriately ephemeral nature. In some cases, permanent, high-quality intervention in a building's fabric may offer a more satisfactory solution in terms of preserving its special architectural interest, especially where overall architectural coherence is a more important criterion than the sensitivity of the building fabric.'[3]

NEW RAMPS AND RAILINGS

Ramps and handrails may generate difficulties when they are added to formal or symmetrical compositions, as the proposed access scheme for the National Westminster Bank in Norwich discussed in Chapter One highlights. These are some of the problems encountered:

- The diagonal line of a ramp may cut across the architectural framework of a symmetrical elevation and unbalance a formal and symmetrical design.
- A diagonal ramp approached along the front of a classically designed building can disrupt an intended axial approach and change the intended hierarchical progression into and through the building.
- Ramps also may diminish the compositional hierarchy reflected in elevated entrances and the historic significance of steps.
- Ramps and handrails may also add visual clutter and may obscure or interfere with original decorative elements and architectural metalwork and railings.

- Fixing ramps and handrails to the existing structure may damage or cause loss of original fabric.

Design strategies

Designers have adopted a variety of techniques and approaches to avoid or correct imbalance caused by new ramps and handrails.

- The slope of the ramp and handrails can be concealed behind a series of horizontal lines. These can be staggered or stepped, often following existing plinth lines to disguise the diagonal slope of the ramp (Figures 4.3, 4.4 and 4.5).
- The introduction of a pair of symmetrical ramps can be used to maintain symmetry, although adding two ramps, when only one is necessary may be prohibitively costly (Figures 3.7, 3.14 and 4.2).
- The visual importance of centrally located steps can be maintained, although the ramp may cut across the front elevation (Figures 4.1 and 4.4).
- Designing and detailing ramps and handrails in materials which harmonize with the existing fabric (Figure 4.5).

Northwich Library

The front elevation of the 1909 Northwich Library, Cheshire, is timber-framed and symmetrical (Figure 4.1). One of the original schemes proposed a long ramp to be located to the centre-left of the main entrance doors in place of a short flight of steps (Figure 4.1(b)). This length of ramp was necessary because of the change of level from the footway to entrance level. The ramp and its off-centre location had the potential effectively to obscure the composition of the main door flanked by two small doors. The scheme was re-worked and retains the concept of a single ramp across the front of the elevation, but in a way which has less impact on the elevation (Figure 4.1(c)).

4.1 Northwich Library, Cheshire.

4.1 (a) Front elevation after alterations.

4.1 (b) Original schematic drawing of proposed ramp to front elevation.

4.1 (c) Revised scheme: this scheme retains more compositional balance. The slope of the ramp is screened by the addition of centre steps placed through the landing area leading to the centre door.

(See page 65.)

(a)

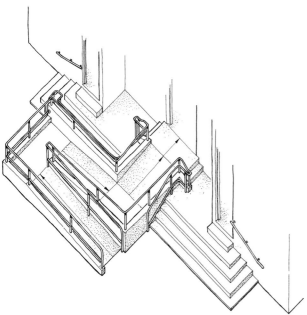

(b)

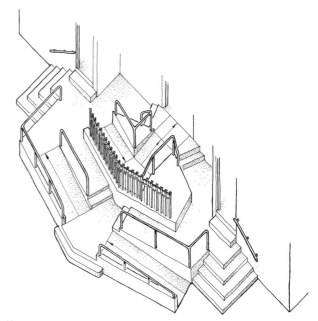

(c)

(a)

4.2 Ashmolean Museum, Oxford.

4.2 (a) Side view of the portico to the front elevation. Historical evidence suggested that the architect conceived his design for the museum while monitoring excavation works in Greece, and that he had intentionally employed what is judged as a revised understanding of the 'Greek temple' form in his design of the main elevation.

4.2 (b) Plan of alterations to the front forecourt by architects Stanton Williams. Access alterations were not made in isolation and were part of a substantial change and updating of existing museum services to improve lecture and study rooms, provide café facilities, and to separate the museum's commercial use from its academic use.

4.2 (c) View of ramped access from the footway through the stone wall leading up to the elevated forecourt.

(c)

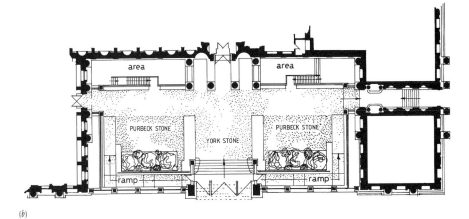

(b)

The Ashmolean Museum

The existing approach to the principal entrance of the Ashmolean Museum, Oxford, was by a flight of steps leading from the footway to the elevated forecourt. The entrance to the building is through the Greek Revival, pedimented portico, slightly raised above the ground level of the forecourt (Figure 4.2). The design of the existing steps, disposition of the handrails and the relationship of the portico to the base were identified as elements of important historic and architectural interest.

An original scheme by architects Stanton Williams called for a radical excavation of the forecourt to create a new, lower ground level entrance, bringing all visitors in through the basement level. The entrance scheme which proposed to change the central architectural features of the elevation drew objections from the conservation authorities who felt that it would clearly have diminished the architectural and historic interest of the building.

Their revised scheme retains the entrance at the forecourt level and maintains the steps on the axis leading to the central doorway within the portico (although visitors now use the side door). The existing steps from the footway are relocated in a forward position into the area of the forecourt. Moving the steps forward from the footway creates a gap at ground level in the balustrade wall. Symmetrical ramps on either side rise from here and traverse inside the front perimeter of the balustrade and then turn along the sides of the forecourt until they reach the raised ground level of the forecourt (Figures 4.2(b) and (c)). Moving the steps resulted in the loss of the original handrails which was an issue opposed in strong protest by the Victorian Society, but was the type of compromise which English Heritage was prepared to accept in order to secure a solution.

THE CRAFTS COUNCIL, LONDON

Occasionally, access schemes can be part of a scheme to reinstate missing elements and for overall repair of building fabric. At the Crafts Council, the design for an access ramp reflected historic precedent as a design inspiration (Figure 4.3). Evidence from historic illustrations showed an original stone balustrade, which had later been removed. The new ramp design uses replacement balustrading to screen the slope of the ramp.

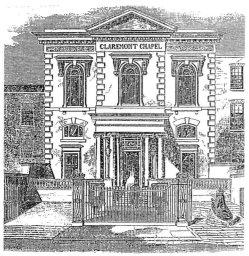

(a)

(b)

4.3 Crafts Council, Camden, London.

4.3 (a) Drawing of original front elevation from historical records.

4.3 (b) Front elevation after alteration to restore balustrade and add access ramps.

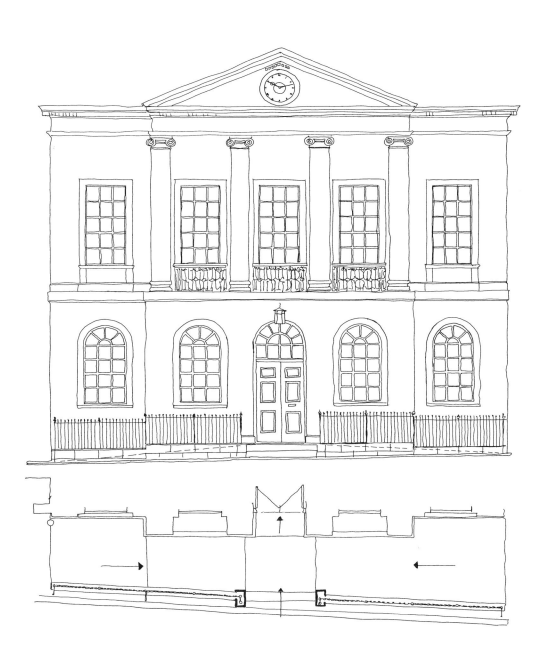

4.4 Ripon Town Hall, Yorkshire.

Front elevation and plan showing alterations.

(*See page* 70.)

PAVEMENT RAMPS

If the space in front of the building is limited or entrance steps lead directly onto the pavement, a *pavement ramp* may provide a solution. This ramp is a permanent structure (as opposed to a portable ramp) in front of a building entrance. It brings the user up to the level of the entrance, making use of the pavement in front of the building entrance.

Although pavement ramps are not intended as a new compositional element, they can make an impact upon symmetry, especially if the building occupies a prominent setting, or if a pavement ramp sits across the main entrance composition.

Ripon Town Hall

Ripon Town Hall, Yorkshire, is a prominent building dating from 1801, by James Wyatt. It occupies a central position on the south side of the Market Square. The front elevation is deliberately symmetrical, with five bays, an attached Ionic portico and a pediment over a rusticated ground floor with arched windows (Figure 4.4). In the design for a pavement ramp in front of the main entrance to Ripon Town Hall, a central bay of steps and the use of symmetrical railings along either side, helps to reinstate and re-emphasize the symmetrical composition.

India Buildings

The pavement ramp added to the front elevation of the India Buildings, in Liverpool, demonstrates a different approach to the design of a ramp occasioned by the setting of the building entrance along the pavement. The ramp is intentionally off-

4.5 India Buildings, Liverpool.

Front elevation showing alteration to the footway for a pavement ramp leading to the building entrance. The choice of materials can affect the way new works harmonize and integrate with existing entrance features. Sympathetic materials in keeping with the original materials, and the adoption of design details which express the horizontal plinth line, may minimize the visual impact of a pavement ramp set before a building.

4.6 Architectural Association, Bedford Square, London.
Rear elevation.

4.7 Manchester Town Hall.
View of handrail added to original entrance steps.

centred and follows the natural rise of the pavement along the street, leading into the enclosed entrance arcade (Figure 4.5). Because the building does not occupy as prominent and visually commanding city centre position as does Ripon Town Hall, there is not the same emphasis on the symmetrical composition and axial intent to the entrance. This makes the building more amenable to an asymmetrical element before the front entrance.

For less important elevations, a simple grading of the existing pavement and the addition of handrails can provide a level route of access (Figure 4.6).

HANDRAILS

A handrail is desirable where there are steps at a principal entrance for use by people with limited mobility and for those

---

PAVEMENT RAMPS: TACTILE SURFACES AND ROAD CLOSURES

Since the pavement ramp encroaches onto the pavement of the public highway it is advisable to provide a tactile warning to alert partially-sighted people to its existence, as was done at India Buildings. Another common issue is whether the ramp over the pavement requires approval from road engineers as a 'street closure'. Where the pavement ramp is designed as a through way, usually with steps or a slope at the far end, it will not be deemed to be a 'street closure'.

(a)

(b)

4.8 Manchester Central Library.

4.8 (a) Front elevation.

4.8 (b) Detail of new ramp and step which extends beyond the existing portico. The tactile surface within the granite is designed to alert blind and partially sighted people to the unexpected steps.

who are partially sighted. Where the location of a ramp at a front entrance is unacceptable, it may be desirable to consider the installation of new handrails (Figure 4.7). The typical issues are again their design and position so as to minimize the visual impact. The addition of handrails can detract from the architectural composition of an existing façade and the fixings can damage existing fabric. Positioning will largely depend on the way the front entrance is designed. Where there is more than one bay of steps it may be preferable to provide a single handrail to either side around the entrance porch, rather than a centre rail.

Handrails are usually also present in ramp schemes, since they are recommended for gradients steeper than 1:20. Even if a proposed ramp may integrate well into the existing composition, the handrails may make the scheme unacceptable.

Manchester Central Library

At Manchester Central Library (Figure 4.8), gentle sloping ramps to either side of the portico provide access from the level of the pavement into the portico. A typical wheelchair user can negotiate the gentle slope without the need for handrails, which

4.9 Bank of England, City of London.

View of interior staircase where a second handrail was added. The design for the new handrails is based on the original wood and iron balustrade.

would have added visual clutter to the façade and detracted from the unique and ornate round form of the building because the ramps extend beyond the form of the portico. The subtle change in level as the gentle ramp approaches the level of the pavement does create a hazard for blind and partially sighted people. To resolve the hazard, as a substitute for handrails, the edge of the ramp is ribbed to provide a tactile surface before the change in level.

Designing new handrails

When new handrails are required for sensitive locations, the design should generally follow that of existing railings. This is generally true for both interior and exterior places (Figure 4.9). There are many exceptions where good new design work departs from any existing precedence (see Figure 1.7). It is also important to consider the recommended criteria for handrail profile, diametre and positioning.

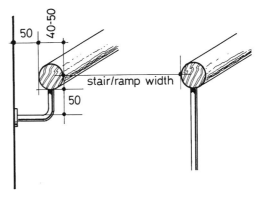

measurements in millimetres

4.10 *Stair and ramp handrail design criteria.*

HANDRAIL STANDARDS

Guidance generally calls for two handrails to either side of steps and a ramp. In some situations, a single continuous handrail may be adequate and less visually intrusive. This compromise works best where the existing porch design allows handrails to be positioned either side of the centre bay of steps, as was done at Liverpool Town Hall (Figure 3.7), thus giving users a choice to use either a left – or right-handed handrail.

Regulations provide guidance on the preferred profile, diameter and positioning (Figure 4.10).

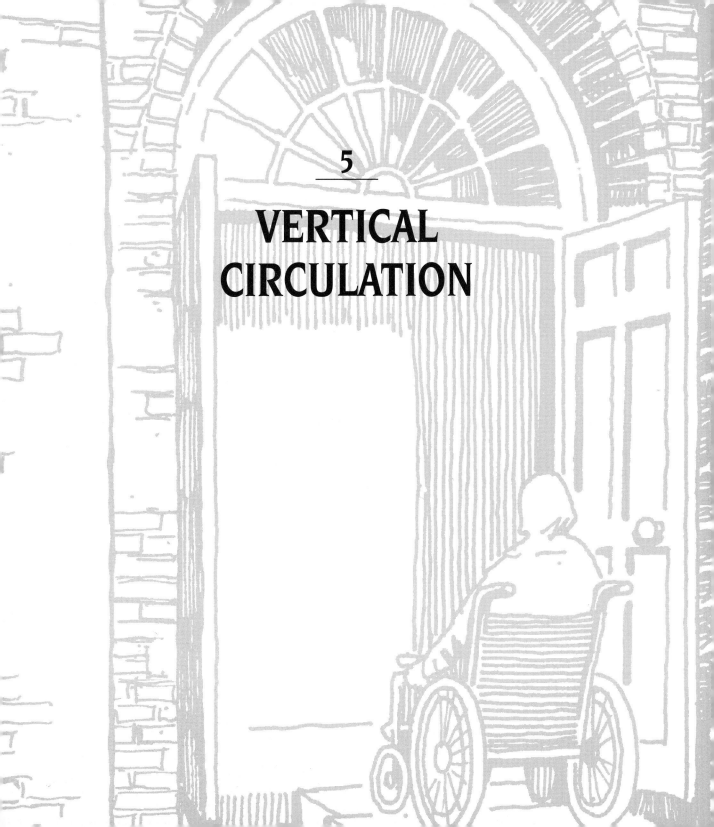

5

VERTICAL CIRCULATION

External and internal vertical circulation for people who cannot negotiate steps often requires the installation of mechanical lift devices. In larger buildings it may be more feasible to plan for the installation of a passenger lift. For smaller properties, wheelchair platform lifts or stair lifts may offer a more viable means of internal level change. Occasionally mechanical lift devices are built externally.

The wheelchair/non-ambulant-dedicated equipment varies in design. Inclined wheelchair platform lifts and stair lifts which may be fitted with a seat, run along the incline of an existing staircase (Figure 5.1). A vertically rising or hydraulic scissor lift is usually situated adjacent to the existing staircase (Figure 5.2). The existing layout and features around a level change will influence which type of equipment will be more useful and appropriate for the building. The design and placement of this type of dedicated equipment can make this equipment far less likely to be used by people who would generally prefer lift access to a stepped route (Figure 5.3); or it can easily integrate

5.1 *Bishop's Gate Institute, London.*
Incline platform lift.

5.2 Tullie House Museum, Carlisle.
Vertical wheelchair platform lift in less important area of the museum provides access to educational rooms. The alterations required a break in the balustrade which gives access onto the lift platform at the top level.

into the setting and be generally available for public use (Figure 5.4).

ACCESS CONSIDERATIONS

When there is a choice of the type of mechanical device to install, passenger lifts are universal-type equipment and can be used by all building users. This added utility will have to be balanced against the additional cost of a passenger lift and the conservation factors. Other considerations include:

- choice of location within sensitive areas and environments;
- the nature of the use, for example, commercial or residential;
- the regularity or familiarity of the users with the controls;
- the level of supervision which might be required.

- **Stair lift or chair lift: this has a seat which travels on a single rail which follow the line of the staircase. The support rails may be mounted on the inside or outside line of the stairs and may be fitted to the stair treads, inside or outside walls or to a balustrade. How the fittings will impact on historic fabric needs to be considered.**
- **Wheelchair platform lift: this has a platform capable of accommodating a wheelchair, which is mounted on continuous support rails following the line of a staircase, and can be mounted like the stair lift support rails. Sometimes the lift is fitted with a seat.**
- **Vertical platform lift: this has a platform which accommodates a wheelchair and which rises via a hydraulic lift; it is freestanding of the staircase.**
- **Part M of the Building Regulations provides guidance on the use of this equipment: sections 2.15 and 2.18. See also, British Standard BS 6440; Part T also refers to BS 6440.**

(a)

(b)

(c)

(d)

There may be other reasons why a platform lift may not be the right access solution.

- As dedicated equipment, largely designed and installed for moving wheelchair users, people tend to be separated from general circulation routes and from their companions.
- The considerable time-delay and unavoidable element of spectacle may also make the equipment less suitable.

- The level of assistance may make the strategy unworkable.

The need for assisted use has been somewhat resolved by a new generation of short rise hydraulic scissor-type lifts. These are less orthopaedic in design and can be independently operated. This type of equipment offers more flexible use, being designed to be more suited to universal use by both wheelchair users and ambulant people. The Musée du Louvre in Paris uses this new

(e)

5.4 *Musée du Louvre, Paris.*

5.4 (*a*), (*b*) and (*c*) Three views of a new generation of lifts designed in a sympathetic manner for a variety of settings within the museum. View (a) shows the full size lift within one bay of steps; view (b) shows the equipment built into the wall; view (c) shows a platform lift adjacent to the staircase. The equipment can be independently operated.

5.4 (*d*) and (*e*) In the Richelieu wing, the new galleries were designed with changes of level and custom-designed lift equipment used without upsetting the interiors of the galleries. View (d) shows how the glass-fronted lift behind a display case harmonizes within the existing interiors; view (e) taken from above shows the discreet nature of the equipment within the interior courtyard.

equipment in the Richelieu wing (Figure 5.4). A similar installation can be found at the Municipal Buildings in Liverpool (Figure 3.15), and at the British Museum, London. Call buttons and controls operate like passenger lifts.

CONSERVATION CONSTRAINTS

Platform lifts are used in historic buildings as a means of achieving both external and internal level changes when mechanical installations may be the only option. When planning for lift installations, the following conservation factors need consideration:

- The importance of the staircase. Staircases are often a principal architectural feature of a historic building and can form part of a formal entrance space. Alteration of any historic staircase is not normally acceptable and it may not be appropriate to add a mechanical device to an important staircase.
- The potential visual impact of the equipment. This depends on the design and location of the existing staircase. A staircase may be carefully designed and of great architectural merit. Or, it may be a plain and massive structure. It may be located in important principal areas or subsidiary circulation routes.
- The potential structural impact. If the staircase is of delicate

5.5 Palm House, Royal Botanic Gardens, Kew.
External platform lift.

construction or of considerable age, strengthening it to take the installation could be damaging visually and structurally.

■ Given the generally phased nature of access works, planning for access to upper floors often follows from proposals for alterations to entrances. If a lift installation will form part of a second phase of works, this should be identified on initial proposals for modification of entrances. This permits conservation authorities to make a full evaluation of the implications for future work that any entrance proposal may have.

PALM HOUSE, ROYAL BOTANIC GARDENS, KEW

An unusual situation has evolved at the Royal Botanic Gardens over the discontinued use of platform lift installed only a few years ago for access to the Marine Biology study area located in the basement below the Palm House (Figure 5.5). For safety reasons, the device must be activated by staff for public operation. Since it is located away from the general circulation route, staff are not in regular attendance, so co-ordination with visitor use proved difficult. The final outcome resulted in the visitor information guide indicating that the area is inaccessible to wheelchair users.

(a)

5.6 St George's Brandon Hill, Bristol.
5.6 (a) Platform lift providing access from elevated car park to entrance level.
5.6 (b) Plan showing alternatives considered for access into the building.

St George's Brandon Hill

A combination of lift installations may provide the most integrated circulation arrangement and have the least impact on historic fabric. St George's Brandon Hill, Bristol, is the home of the St George's Music Trust and has become a busy performance and recording centre. During the third stage of the conversion project, the Architectural Heritage Fund, together with other donors including ADAPT, one of the charities specializing in access grants for arts venues, provided funding for access works as part of an overall refurbishment and conversion scheme (Figure 5.6).

Architects, Ferguson Mann, proposed five alternative access options to overcome the down-and-up nature of access from the upper level car park to the main public areas (Figure 5.6(b)). The options were considered in the following way. Routes A, D

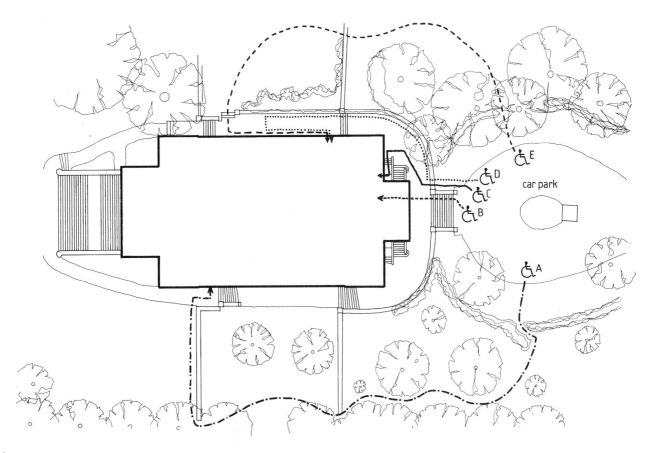

(b)

and E avoided mechanical lifts but had other problems. The travel distance for wheelchairs was too long and the necessary changes to the landscape were unacceptable. Route A was through an existing stage entrance, while D and E necessitated opening up a new entry. All routes compromised user integration since they were so far off the general circulation route.

Route B, which relies on two platform lifts, involved no structural work, is direct and is adjacent to the principal entrance. But its location on a general circulation route had

5.7 Terraced House, Westminster, London.

Front elevation showing platform lift over basement area.

(a)

(b)

5.8 Ranger's House, Greenwich, London.

5.8 (*a*) Front elevation.

5.8 (*b*) Side elevation showing location of platform lift: to facilitate use, signs should indicate the location of parking and the accessible entrance. A bell or intercom device and remote security camera adjacent to the lift is desirable to alert staff where assistance is required. While in practice disabled people tend to make advance arrangements, and family members or an attendant can locate staff, this cannot always be assumed.

other problems; visual impact of the equipment and the risk of the installations obstructing emergency egress.

The preferred route C had the advantage of being closest to the main entrance without obstructing it. Impact on existing fabric was considered to be minimal, although it obstructs a secondary fire escape route from the building.

The following illustrations show how some installations have been added in a variety of external and internal settings (Figures 5.7–5.11).

PASSENGER LIFTS

When vertical circulation can be achieved via a passenger lift this will be most used by the general public, serving the needs of far more people than just wheelchair users. This can be an important consideration when budgeting for access improvements. Passenger lifts can also achieve a greater degree of user integration which is not possible with dedicated equipment like the platform lifts which may require separate routes to avoid sensitive areas.

5.9 The Royal Society, Carleton Terrace, Westminster, London.

5.10 The Royal Opera House, Covent Garden.

Platform lift inside main entrance foyer. Wheelchair installations such as this platform lift can provide access as an interim solution while a long-term strategy is worked out as part of an overall site redevelopment.

Conservation considerations include:

- The sensitivity of the floor frame which would have to be cut through by a lift shaft. If the fabric is of eighteenth century or an earlier date then the floor structure needs to be investigated. Decorated beams and ceilings or massive plain beams of an early date should be preserved.
- The need for a machinery pit, which has archaeological implications in the ground disturbance beneath the building.

- The external implication of the lift over-run, which requires head-room above the top of the lift shaft. This may require alterations to the roof structure.

Fan Museum

The Fan Museum, Greenwich, occupies the lower floors of two converted Georgian terraced houses, number 10 and number necessitated rebuilding of the areas as part of the conversion/conservation works. This rebuilding afforded the opportunity to add a new lift shaft (Figure 5.12(b)). The museum estimates that providing the lift added about four per cent to its costs but notes that the lift has added value in helping to move displays, providing access to the flats – benefits which are not included in this cost assessment.

Thorpe Hall

When Peterborough City Council first assumed responsibility for Thorpe Hall they intended to convert the building to a community-based cultural facility. Subsequently, the Council agreed to pass the building on to the Sue Ryder Foundation for use as a long-term hospice facility. When the property was under the control of the Council, a passenger lift had been installed. When the Foundation took over the building, the existing lift had to be enlarged to accommodate bed-patients.

The original lift installation was designed as a free-standing element within one quadrant of the existing building layout (Figure 5.13). This works as a self-contained, free-standing installation, avoiding the need to alter or demolish interior features which contribute to the special interest of the interiors, although the location would require loss of structural floor members.

When the hospice took over use of the building, the need to enlarge the lift shaft to accommodate beds exacerbated the original loss, but the increased dimension was contained within the quadrant without alteration to interior features. This highlights how a proposed change of use of this type can impose specialized access requirements which must be reconciled with the overall care and maintenance of the building. Decisions on change of use are made in the context of the overall planning process for listed buildings, which favours finding compatible new uses rather than keeping buildings of this type as museum pieces.

When local authority conservation officers and conservation bodies like English Heritage must evaluate change of use

5.11 Bishop's Palace, Ely.

A platform lift for hospice patient use when changing floors is located within a void between floors. In making use of the void, the existing historic panelling was altered to provide an opening on the lower floor level. The non-public nature of this access gave designers, Freeland Rees-Roberts, more flexibility in planning circulation routes.

12, Crooms Hill, with residential accommodation on the top floors (Figure 5.12). The houses were built in 1727 and are Grade II* listed. The original staircase could not be altered so a lift was proposed for vertical circulation, to serve both public visitors to the museum and to improve access to the upper floor flats. The importance of the houses made finding a suitable location for the new lift shaft challenging. After extensive negotiations with English Heritage, it was finally agreed that a new lift shaft could be added to the rear elevation of number 10. Extensive dry rot damage which had been detected in the area,

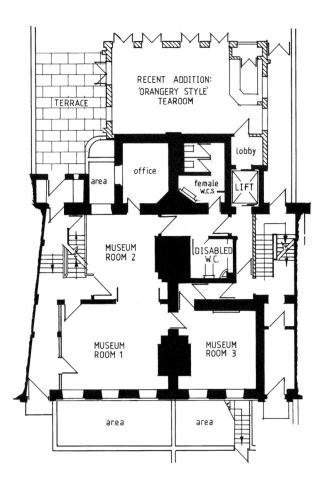

(a)

(b)

5.12 Fan Museum, Greenwich, London.

5.12 (a) Plan showing location of new lift.

5.12 (b) Rear elevation showing new lift shaft constructed in brick.

(See page 84.)

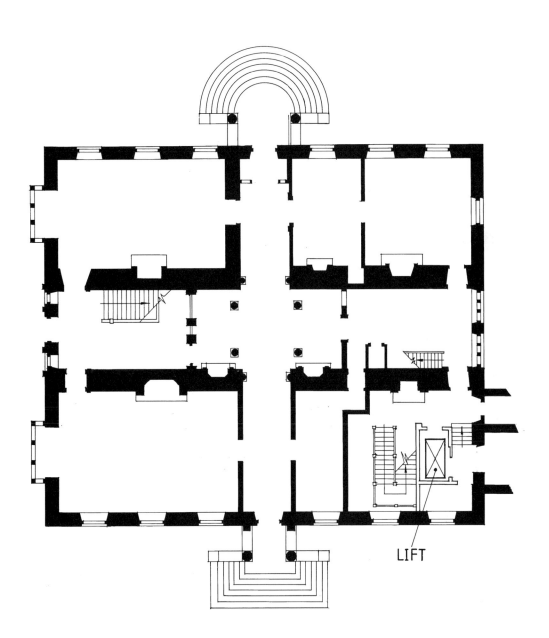

LIFT

**5.13 Thorpe Hall,
Peterborough.**

Plan showing location of lift
used for bed-patients in a
hospice care facility.

(*See page* 85.)

proposals, the objective is to strike a balance between the benefit of finding a suitable new use and minimizing the need for physical alteration.

Colchester Castle

The structure of Colchester castle is mostly Norman, constructed between 1076 and 1125 (Figure 5.14). The structure is a scheduled ancient monument and therefore subject to more restrictive legislation. The castle was originally built as a defensible structure and continued in use as a prison until the nineteenth century. There has been a museum in part of the building since 1860. In the 1930s major additions were made and the keep was roofed over to create a substantial new museum gallery space on two floors. A 1991 Museum Development Plan set out a realistic programme of improvements over a five-year period, including the provision of lift access to the upper galleries. The lift shaft has been sited centrally to cut

(a)

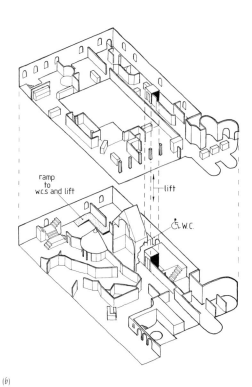

(b)

5.14 Colchester Castle Museum.

5.14 (a) Main visitor's entrance.

5.14 (b) Plan showing location of lift.

through a 1930s floor avoiding alteration to the remaining Norman structure (Figure 5.14(b)). The lift pit proved more difficult, as it had to be located into the original Castle floor. A full archaeological excavation was carried out before the motor pit could be finally approved and installed.

Motorized mobility devices

As a last resort, where structural barriers cannot be changed or overcome with a lift installation, a free-standing mobility device can provide wheelchair access to upper floors. One type of device is known as a scaliamobile. This motorized device attaches to the wheelchair to allow a helper to move the visitor up or down a staircase (Figure 5.15). The National Trust, which has a positive policy against carrying, uses it when the building cannot be suitably altered. At the Queen Elizabeth's Hunting Lodge in Epping Forest, Essex, this device is available for access to the upper floors since the scheduled ancient monument is too sensitive to admit a lift (see Chapter Six).

Where these devices are used, access in this manner may be the only means of enabling wheelchair users to get in or get around, short of carrying, and the only means of integrating visitors with disabilities into otherwise inaccessible programmes and tours.

In practice the utility of these motorized devices for public use appears limited. They tend to fit only older, standard-issue chairs and are cumbersome for both staff and the wheelchair users. Volunteer staff report that they would rather not assume responsibility for the safety of a wheelchair user in this way and wheelchair users report that they would rather forego the visit than be hauled around in this manner. In the end this access solution is an extreme compromise of the dignity and independence of disabled people.

Another argument against use of the these mobility devices is that access in this manner can be a deterrent to making more permanent alterations. Although mobility devices may become a *crutch* for owners to avoid the issue of independent access, this argument must be evaluated in terms of the building's function.

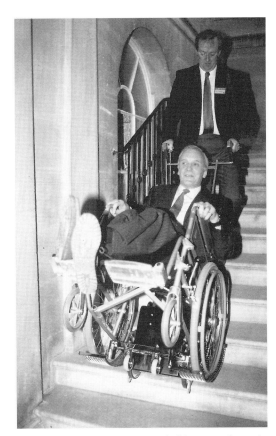

5.15 A motorized device for moving wheelchairs, Osterley Park, a National Trust property.

At public and commercial buildings, the function and use of the building dictates a greater degree of independence than these devices can offer, so their use should be avoided except for short-term temporary solutions. Where the priority issue is preservation of the architecture, as with cultural monuments, like historic country houses, which function as museums, this sort of compromise in favour of the cultural value of the architecture *may* be more justified. It is a reality that a conservative approach to access to cultural monuments may necessitate less independence for the disabled visitor than would be appropriate or desirable at public buildings, like a town hall. If one accepts that the use of these mobility devices is more dignified than carrying, then their use as an access solution for wheelchair users must be viewed as a compromise in favour of protecting the cultural value of the architecture. Not everyone accepts this view.

6

CULTURAL
MONUMENTS

COUNTRY HOUSES, RUINS AND LANDSCAPES

This chapter is concerned with access to areas of cultural interest: country houses and places associated with important historic figures or events; scheduled ancient monuments like the structures and archaeological ruins of abbeys and priories; castles and battle fortifications; and historic landscapes and gardens. The majority of monuments are places of leisure and recreation for the public, although these places may also provide research facilities for historians and scholars and are important archaeological records. The monument and its setting has generally ceased to develop beyond a certain date and in some cases interpretation may actually remove later accretions and reinstate features to an earlier period.

As places of aesthetic, historic, scientific and social value for past, present and future generations, their continued maintenance – usually at public expense – directly or through grant aid, is linked to national and local identity and a sense of the past. While working buildings often undergo extensive change and alteration to keep them in use, the role and significance of cultural monuments dictate a different approach. They are museum pieces and as such, interpretation and leisure activities have mostly replaced the building's economic use.

There are strong national and international conservation standards in legislation and through agreed practices which aim to maintain the fabric of a cultural monument without change. The Ancient Monuments and Archaeological Areas Act of 1979 invokes a strong presumption against *any* change to the original fabric. Important listed buildings are also protected from the type of changes which occur to working buildings when there has been a decision to provide the financial means for the care and maintenance for the building through means other than continued economic use.

Works to these types of buildings are generally limited and done for the specific purpose of protection of the original fabric. In some instances restoration may be appropriate to return the site to an earlier known existing state, either by removing accretions or by reassembling existing components. In extreme cases reconstruction may involve the introduction of new or old materials into the existing fabric. Either situation is not intended to record a new period along the monument's historic time line. Consequently, changes to accommodate visitor use are done with less permanency and less intervention.

Same objectives, more compromises

The access aim at cultural monuments is to provide disabled visitors with the same enjoyment and appreciation of the monument or site – and in the same manner – as other visitors. This means aiming for independence and integration. Independent and integrated access allows the disabled visitor to explore the site at his or her own pace, without the need for assistance or the stigma of a separate route just for disabled people. Freedom and choice to explore a site are important visitor concepts when planning for any visitor, including the disabled visitor. These objectives can be part of the planning and design of facilities for disabled people. Information about the building or site is a key element in planning for disabled visitors; a practice refined by the National Trust.

There are, however, more compromises on circulation at monuments than at working buildings. Disabled people generally accept these compromises, in recognition of the national interest in promoting conservation. Independence is one of the areas of compromise, which occurs naturally because of the higher level of custodial and volunteer staff in public areas. Family members and friends can also provide assistance, as to some extent monuments are places of leisure enjoyed in the company of others. Integration is another area of compromise, with changed circulation routes and limited access sometimes being necessary. This may change the way a person in a wheelchair will experience a site, through a changed circulation route. This alternative route may start with a temporary ramp at the side entrance. There may be limited access to areas on the level and no access to areas where there are level changes. Limited access or changed routes are more acceptable if there has been enough access to principal rooms and collections to convey the importance of the site. Similarly, limited access can sometimes be supplemented through the use of interpretative materials. When deciding about compromises, the provision of access should permit a meaningful experience.

If full access to all parts of a structure or site may not be possible, *access through interpretation* or providing interpretation of the inaccessible areas may help link accessible areas to those inaccessible spaces. However interpretation is not a substitute for physical access. Why else make the visit? Interpretation in this context should be seen to supplement physical access not substitute for it.

The reason interpretation is not enough is that visiting the monument or site is the essence of the experience – being there and exploring. This means getting in and moving around.

Because of the priority to protect historic fabric, there is usually little scope for permanent structural alterations to the main entrances and rooms. Means of access may be through temporary ramps which remain in place through the opening season, or through managed ramps which are put in place when needed. Temporary ramps may be located away from principal circulation routes, such as at a side entrance. Occasionally a mechanical lift device like the wheelchair platform lift may be fitted at less important entrance points or on less sensitive interior circulation routes. One exception is the platform lift fitted to the front elevation of Harewood House, Yorkshire (Figure 6.1). The most improvement and physical change occurs in the provision of accessible catering facilities and WCs, especially when these are located in less sensitive areas of the site. However, as with all historic properties, it will be the unique opportunities and limitations of a site which will determine in part the opportunity to provide an accessible route. Blickling Hall, a National Trust property in Norfolk, is one example where the provision of a passenger lift in the existing turret had no visible impact on the special architectural interest and resulted in no significant loss of historic fabric (Figure 6.7). Visitor centres and buildings of lesser historic interest although listed or within the

ACCESS THROUGH INTERPRETATION

The objection to interpretation as a form of access is that some building owners and managers will leave a picture book or an interactive 3-D video at the front, inaccessible entrance as a substitute for a meaningful experience. Interpretative material should clarify that it is not intended to be a substitute for physical access. The legitimate aim of access through interpretation should be to facilitate greater enjoyment and understanding of a site when physical access is limited by conservation constraints.

setting of the historic property can also offer alternative locations for accessible WCs.

The National Trust (England and Wales and Northern Ireland)

Charitable bodies like the National Trusts of England and Wales, Northern Ireland, and that of Scotland play important

HAREWOOD HOUSE
Harewood House is located on the Harewood estate, in West Yorkshire (Figure 6.1). The front façade is by John Carr, the south elevation remodelled by Sir Charles Barry and the interiors are the art of Robert Adam. Visitors enter the house through the main entrance and all visitor circulation is on the ground floor. The entrance rises up from the grounds' several steps. Initial plans for a temporary ramp to be located on the side elevation were drawn up, but after consideration, the ramp structure, even though temporary in nature, was considered too great a visual impact on the building's special interest. The compromise solution is a plain, undecorated wheelchair platform lift installed on the porch at the front elevation. The use of platform lifts at principal exterior elevations, especially for buildings of this type is unusual, yet one can appreciate that the device is far less visually intrusive than a massive temporary ramp extending several metres into the setting before the building (Figure 6.1(b)). The massive scale of the formal elevation and the absence of efforts to disguise the device helps minimize the visual intrusion. Visually, it does not become part of the architectural composition of the elevation in the way a semi-permanent ramp would.

(a)

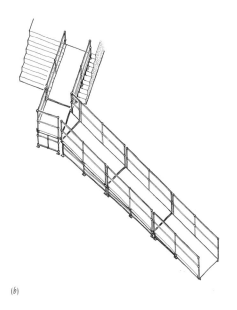

(b)

(c)

6.1 Harewood House, Yorkshire.

6.1 (a) Front elevation.

6.1 (b) Proposed temporary ramp to front elevation.

6.1 (c) View of platform lift installed on main porch.

(See page 93.)

roles in the historic environment because of their vast owner-ship and control over a large number of historic houses, gardens, and areas of open countryside. The principal role of these bodies is to protect the buildings and their settings and open them to the public for enjoyment. Buildings and sites under their care are usually cultural monuments; their care and upkeep is no longer linked to economic use of the site in the way continued use of a working building may be.

Because funding for charitable bodies comes from public sources, the provision of access for disabled people falls within the mandate that public bodies make their properties available to the nation. This has been the policy of the National Trust for England and Wales. The Trust estimates that 25–30 per cent of its visitors have some disability or infirmity which affects enjoyment of a Trust property. The increasing emphasis on access considerations has been one of cause and effect, in that both the attitudes of the Trust and its visitors to the need and acceptance of limited change are evolving. In the not too distant past, Trust properties were viewed as inaccessible by people with physical disabilities. As access improvements have been made, especially the provision of accessible WCs, disabled people have change their notion of the National Trust as a place of inaccessibility to one of accessibility.

An important tool in this process of change is the information guide which has been published annually since 1978. This gives information about the buildings and site access, and accessible facilities, allows visitors to decide whether to visit a site and how to prepare for a visit. Individual site guides provide more detailed information about accessible routes, barriers and assistance, and the Trust encourages visitors to telephone properties for detailed information.

The National Trust access policy provides a typical framework of an 'access for all' approach to visitor care:

> The National Trust welcomes visitors with disabilities to its properties ... [and] wishes to integrate visitors with disabilities with other visitors and must somehow steer a course through the requirements for many people with vastly differing disabilities. It is not possible to provide exactly the right facilities for everyone, so the Trust concentrates on easing access for more severely disabled people: including those in wheelchairs. If they are able to enjoy a property, it usually follows that more ambulant people will also have a comfortable visit.[4]

With its vast portfolio of properties, the Trust has aimed to improve access through a systematic scheme of assessment, recommendations, then reassessment, region by region, under the supervision of Mrs Valerie Wenham, full time Adviser for Disabled Visitors. The implementation of access improvements on her recommendation and under her supervision has shown that over time, access comes about because of a growing awareness and change in culture which accepts the needs of disabled people as a legitimate conservation concern. Her experience over the past years has shown that what may have been considered inappropriate or unobtainable at National Trust properties has changed considerably from when the programme commenced in the 1970s, and will continue to do so as attitudes continue to change.

This shift in attitude comes about in part because more intervention and change *is* acceptable. But equally important is the acceptance that although a disabled person may have a *different* experience from what an able-bodied visitor sees or experiences, the visit can still be a meaningful one.

CIRCULATION STRATEGIES

Approach

Practices for visitor parking vary, largely depending on the site layout. Administrative practices usually allow a drop-off point which is signposted or marked on visitor information guides.

Some sites allow disabled drivers to park in front of the main entrance, which would not be allowed for others.

Setting

An existing cobbled or gravel setting can present a barrier and be difficult or painful for many others to use. At Gawthorpe Hall in Lancashire, an extensive scheme set paving stones into the cobbles to create a stable footpath through the yard (Figure 6.2). For short distances, increasing the mortar in joints can create a short level route through a cobbled or sett area (Figure 6.3). Gravel footpaths in gardens are another area of concern, with gravel increasingly being replaced by other natural quarried materials which offer a stable surface.

FOOTPATH SURFACING

At Beningbrough Hall, Yorkshire, the National Trust has been experimenting with materials and construction methods for footpaths which are an alternative to gravel, but maintain the character of the setting.

Adequate drainage can be a key consideration, since some surfacing materials which are stable in dry weather can turn to sludge in wet weather. Beningbrough Hall uses Breedon quarry gravel because of its creamy brown colour which blends in well with the existing landscape but it tends to puddle in wet weather. To enhance drainage over the clay surface, the gravel is laid over a bed of rolled limestone rubble. A rubble core is preferable to other drainage techniques such as chamfering the path.

6.2 *Gawthorpe Hall, Lancashire.*

York stone paviors provide an accessible route through the cobbled yard leading into the site.

6.3 Cardiff Castle, Wales.

Increasing the mortar between cobble setts can create a short accessible path; for longer routes it is advisable to consider laying paving stones through the cobbles or setts to provide a stable and accessible route as was done at Gawthorpe Hall (Figure 6.2).

Getting in

Grand elevated stepped entrances are a common feature of many historic houses. If this entrance is the principal way in, it may be necessary to find an alternative route. The use of a semi-permanent temporary ramp at a side entrance is one common practice. At many houses, the general visitor circulation route begins at some other point which may be more manageable.

Where the number of steps is not too great, some sites use a managed portable ramp which is set up by staff when needed, and removed after use. The higher level of staffing or volunteers available makes the use of managed ramps more feasible.

Flexible circulation

Greater flexibility in visitor circulation can be more appropriate for places of leisure than for working buildings. If lifts or ramps are not feasible for level changes, a changed circulation route may be another option. This is one strategy adopted by the National Trust.

(a)

6.4 Trerice, Cornwall.

6.4 (a) and (b) Original and altered cobbled path to rear entrance. Paving stones were laid to create a firm and stable route suitable for wheelchair users.

6.4 (c) View of side entrance to first floor for visitors who cannot negotiate steps.

6.4 (d) Plan from National Trust visitors guide shows route from car park to accessible entrance route access to the side entrance for viewing of upper floors and location of accessible WC.

(b)

(c)

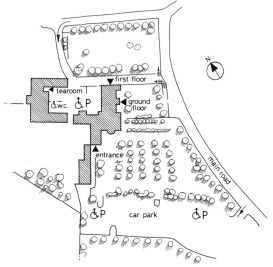

(d)

6.5 Ham House, Richmond.

The visually intrusive temporary ramp is too steep to be used independently and could pose a safety risk because of the lack of handrails.

Trerice

Trerice in Cornwall, is a rare surviving example of an Elizabethan manor house. High walls enclose a small turfed entrance court in front of the E-shaped façade (Figure 6.4). The house can be approached from the main entrance but this includes several steps. An alternative, accessible entrance is located at the back court, avoiding the steps (Figure 6.4(a)). This links easily with designated parking in the adjacent car park and is closer to facilities like the WC and café located in the Great Barn.

The main visitor circulation areas are on the ground and first floors. Stepped access provides the only means of access to the upper rooms. Visitors who cannot negotiate steps but wish to view first floors rooms can exit the house where they came in, and travel along the outside to the bowling green from where it is possible to re-enter at the first floor level (Figure 6.4(c)). This

TEMPORARY RAMPS

When temporary ramps are used, they should be designed with two objectives in mind: suitability for intended use and visual impact on the setting. Temporary ramps are often too steep for independent use or require too great an effort for those helping. In the wrong location they have an adverse visual impact (Figures 6.5 and 6.6).

6.6 Holyrood Palace, Edinburgh.

The temporary ramp has handrails and a short rise suitable for independent use.

(*See page* 99.)

6.7 *Blickling Hall, Norfolk.*

Front elevation showing turret where lift is discreetly located.

side door access is not on the general circulation route, and is not left open without assistance being available. This alternative circulation route is marked on a site guide (Figure 6.4(d)).

Blickling Hall

Blickling Hall is one of the greatest houses in East Anglia dating from the early seventeenth century (Figure 6.7). A key feature of the house is the Jacobean plaster ceiling in the long gallery on the first floor, making access to the first floor a priority. A lift has been located in the non-public area of one of the turrets. Use of this void means that the lift does not impact on important historic fabric or the visual aspects of the exterior interior. This is an example of exploiting the opportunities which may exist at a particular site. The tour route is adapted for disabled visitors, although in general, visitors follow the same route. All visitors enter through the main entrance. Because of the threshold steps, a temporary ramp is in place. The temporary ramp could have been avoided by routing wheelchair users around to a side entrance adjacent to the lift,

(a)

(b)

6.8 Queen Elizabeth's Hunting Lodge, Epping Forest, Essex.

6.8 (a) The level route at the front entrance allows visitors who cannot negotiate steps to enjoy exhibits and displays on the ground level.

6.8 (b) Handrails were added to the ancient staircase.

but the National Trust follows a strategy, wherever possible, to ensure that all visitors use the same route. This practice benefits integrated visitor circulation and eases the burden on room stewards. Kitchen areas and a few minor rooms of the main house remain inaccessible.

Inaccessible sites

Some sites may be extremely difficult to adapt for visitors who cannot negotiate steps. For inaccessible properties it may be possible to focus interpretative efforts towards accessible areas elsewhere, and to do more for visitors with other disabilities.

Queen Elizabeth's Hunting Lodge

The Queen Elizabeth's Hunting Lodge in Epping Forest, Essex was built for Henry VIII as a great 'stonedeinge' or grandstand to watch the hunt on Chingford Plain (Figure 6.8). The structure was completed in 1543 and is now a Scheduled Ancient Monument. The main viewing areas on the upper floors look out across the forest where the hunt took place. The viewing areas are inaccessible to those who cannot negotiate steps. Installation of a passenger lift or other mechanical lift device was not feasible because of the historic importance of the surviving structure. Wheelchair users can request assisted access to the upper floors if they are brave enough to allow staff to assist with

6.9 Castle Howard, Yorkshire.

Chair lift for ambulant visitors who cannot negotiate the steep steps leading to the main floor.

a scaliamobile (see Figure 5.15). Not surprisingly, few wheelchair users will use this method to go up the winding staircase.

Wheelchair users and others who cannot negotiate steps are encouraged to visit the ground floor of the Lodge, where interpretative panels explain the history of the site and the method of construction. Through this interpretation, the site becomes a meaningful experience, despite the lack of physical access to the upper floors.

Although there is limited wheelchair access, it was still possible to improve access for ambulant people by providing handrails along the staircase leading to the viewing rooms (Figure 6.8(b)).

Castle Howard

Castle Howard, Yorkshire, offers another example illustrating how access can be improved for ambulant visitors, although the upper floors are inaccessible to wheelchair users. A chair lift provides access up a steep staircase leading to the principal rooms on the first floor (Figure 6.9). The chair lift is regularly used by older people and others who have difficulty negotiating steps.

UNROOFED MONUMENTS AND HISTORIC LANDSCAPES

Unroofed monuments and historic landscapes are discovery-oriented sites. Visitors are encouraged to explore the site and ruins at their own pace usually through the aid of a site map. Disabled visitors can use a site guide to locate barriers and plan accessible routes, or they explore the site at their leisure without following a pre-planned route. When a barrier is encountered, the site guide can indicate an alternative route. In this way access to the monument maintains the same sense of exploration for the wheelchair user as exists for other visitors.

Unroofed monuments

The archaeological sensitivity above and below ground of unroofed structures and monuments, requires a practice of minimal intervention when planning a circulation route. Existing barriers such as the remains of walls and thresholds are deliberately preserved in their original state. The key is to find a means around the barriers without physical intervention. There

> **WICKET GATES**
>
> **Livestock graze the site, requiring wicket or 'kissing' gates, which can be a particular problem for some disabled people and parents with prams. Gates can be designed to meet the minimum dimension criteria to be usable by someone in a wheelchair (Figure 6.10(a)).**

is more scope, depending on the site, to add handrails, lighting fixtures and interpretative boards or directional signs.

Two approaches: Bolton Abbey and Hailes Abbey

Bolton Abbey and Hailes Abbey share a conservative philosophy of minimal physical intervention. This is consistent with

(a)

(b)

6.10 Bolton Abbey, Yorkshire.

6.10 (a) The modified wicket gate designed by The Fieldfare Trust, Sheffield, is accessible to wheelchair users and parents with children in prams.

6.10 (b) Where the natural slope of the terrain is too steep for easy access, viewing points provide an alternative means of enjoyment.

the general approach to visitor enjoyment of sensitive archaeological sites required under the Scheduled Ancient Monuments and Archaeological Areas of Act. Intervention or alteration is kept to a minimum except where necessary to preserve the condition of original fabric. For visitors with disabilities, the principal difference is the way circulation strategies have been approached.

Bolton Abbey and Strid Wood

Bolton Abbey, Yorkshire, is located on the estate of the Duke of Devonshire, adjacent to historic Strid Wood. The approach emphasizes exploration with the aid of a site map, keeping signage to a minimum. A wheelchair visitor may encounter many thresholds between the remains of rooms within the priory ruins, making some areas inaccessible. This is not seen as a problem, since the exploratory nature of the site provides alternative routes. Formal pathways do not exist. In normal summer weather conditions, a natural surface grass does not present a barrier if properly maintained.

Bolton Abbey is adjacent to the Strid Wood Nature Trail. The access strategy adopted for the monument extends into this area of scenic beauty, keeping intrusive signage to a minimum. A colour-coded guidebook explains to visitors the choice of routes available and allows the visitor to choose which route best suits their level of strength and ability. Here it was possible

6.11 Hailes Abbey, Gloucestershire.

Information panel set within the monument for easy enjoyment by visitors in wheelchairs.

6.12 *Stourhead, Wiltshire.*

Ambulant visitors with limited mobility can visit the historic gardens and landscapes of Stourhead. Re-graded footpaths through the historic gardens avoid steep steps and slopes.

(*See page* 106.)

to make some improvements: provide seating, and stabilize and widen footpaths to 1.5 m so that wheelchair users and their companions can remain side-by-side. The easy access route is marked with a friendly hand pointing the easiest way forward. This subtle approach avoids the stigma of disability associated with signing which is only for wheelchair users. For inaccessible areas, viewing points can be constructed (Figure 6.10(b)).

Hailes Abbey

Hailes Abbey, Gloucestershire, is the scheduled ruins of the thirteenth-century Cistercian Abbey (Figure 6.11). The site is managed by English Heritage. In 1992 the Education Department developed a series of information panels linked to an audio tour to bring the Abbey ruins to life by giving an impression of how the monks lived, how the various rooms looked and how they were used nearly 500 years ago. The tape offers visitors the option of a more structured circulation route if desired. The format and length of the tapes vary according to an individual's ability. A longer 45-minute version explores the entire site in the greatest detail and a shorter version offers wheelchair users and older visitors an easier route. A third tape is designed specifically for visually-impaired visitors. All of the tapes can be used with an induction loop which is provided free of charge.

6.13 Castle Howard, Yorkshire.

A subtle alteration made to the grassy lawn creates a gentle sloping route around existing steps in the land-scaped terrace.

6.13 Castle Howard, Yorkshire.

A subtle alteration made to the grassy lawn creates a gentle sloping route around existing steps in the landscaped terrace.

In planning the visitor information scheme it was important not to spoil the special atmosphere of the place. The scheme included the provision of a new mown grass footpath around the perimeter of the ruins linking the new audiotape with the information panels. The panels are placed at a comfortable height and angle for wheelchair users, between 1000 mm and 1500 mm.

Historic landscapes and gardens

Landscapes and gardens form an important part of the historic environment, often providing the setting for historic houses or other important historic buildings and structures. Access to gardens and landscapes can play an important role in enhancing a disabled visitors's enjoyment of a site, especially where the house or other built structure has limited access. A key component of access schemes is discreet signing within the landscape to ensure that disabled people can find accessible entrances via the service routes, without detracting from the visual aesthetics of the landscape (Figures 6.12 and 6.13).

The Royal Botanic Gardens, Kew

Kew Gardens is one of the world's pre-eminent botanical gardens with a history of visitor enjoyment dating back 150 years. Accommodating visitors, especially older visitors has long been a part of the culture of Kew so it was natural to extend this philosophy to meet the needs of disabled visitors. An

6.14 *The Royal Botanic Garden, Kew.*

Ramps originally constructed for garden maintenance can form natural access routes.

important aspect of the access philosophy is the assumption that disabled people visit Kew with friends, family and attendants. As noted in Chapter One, this offers an approach where assistance for disabled visitors is part of the access strategy rather than merely a physical alteration. In the context of another setting, such as in the workplace or public buildings like a town hall, this restriction on independence could result in seriously compromising the disabled person's independence. Understanding how the site is visited and the actual needs of visitors can help clarify the compromises that might be made, without reducing a person's enjoyment.

Aspects of Kew's terrain make the garden readily accessible for wheelchair and ambulant, disabled visitors, because the landscape is relatively flat and open. The concentration of the

FOOTPATH CONSTRUCTION

Surfacing on footways should be firm, even and not become slippery when wet.

- **The cross fall should not exceed 2.5 per cent.**
- **The edge should be defined by a kerb of 100 mm or a distinct change in texture, such as grass or gravel.**
- **Handrails provide effective assistance for wheelchair users, ambulant people and those with visual impairments.**

main visitor interests in the centre and at the north end of the Gardens, facilitates circulation for those with physical limitations to many of the visitor sites. For longer distances into the woodland areas of the Gardens, where pathways could be more difficult for wheelchair users (especially on wetter days) an anonymous donor has commissioned the architect Sir Norman Foster to develop a prototype mobility bus to take wheelchair and less-able visitors from the visitor centre to the outer garden areas.

Specific access routes have grown organically out of the development of the Gardens over the past 150 years and service and maintenance vehicle ramps have been introduced into the landscape over time. These routes can form natural alternative routes around the more formal stepped approaches to the structure like the Temperate House and the Palm House. In one instance where conservation work has been undertaken at the Waterlily House, the service route has been redesigned to form an integrated accessible approach as part of the landscape (Figure 6.14).

APPENDIX
PRACTICAL GUIDANCE

1. WHEELCHAIR SIZE AND CLEARANCES REQUIRED

1.1 Size of chair

When planning for accessibility it is best to make provision for the larger models of electrically powered wheelchairs whose overall dimensions are approximately 675 mm wide and 1150 mm long.

1.2 Turning radius

A space of 1400 mm by 1400 mm is required for a standard wheelchair to turn through 90° and 1400 mm by 1800 mm to turn through 180°. As part of a circulation route, a wheelchair can make a 90° turn within a minimum corridor or passage width of 900 mm.

2. ENTRANCE DOORS AND LOBBIES

2.1 Clearance

Accessible entrance doors into a building must provide clear access of 800 mm and respect the dimensional and other requirements for entrance lobbies as illustrated in Part M of the Building Regulations. Automatic sliding doors are preferable.

2.2 Controls and communications

Easily accessible controls are required as well as a communication system (call for assistance) between the outside and the reception inside where necessary.

2.3 Colour and finish

Entrance doors should be easily identifiable to partially sighted persons.

3. INTERIOR DOORS

3.1 Door width

Regulations require that interior doors provide a clear opening of at least 750 mm, with 800 mm clear width being preferred.

3.2 Clear space

A clear space at least 300 mm wide is required adjacent to the leading edge of a door (out of the door swing space) to permit unaided opening from a wheelchair position.

3.3 Vision panels

Doors crossing circulation corridors must have a glazed vision panel providing a zone of visibility from a height of 900 mm to 1500 mm above FFL (finished floor level). Entry doors to certain heavily occupied or used rooms (such as seminar rooms, meeting rooms and waiting rooms) should also have glazed panels.

3.4 Ironmongery

Doors should have ironmongery chosen for visibility and ease of operation. Lever type handles are preferred. Door closers should require minimum pressure to operate, be slow in operation and be equipped with stay-open mechanisms. Where fire safety permits, kick plates 400 mm high will protect doors against wheelchair damage.

4. INTERIOR CORRIDORS

4.1 Minimum width

Interior corridors must provide an unobstructed width of 1200 mm.

4.2 Colour and finishes

Excessively monochromatic colour schemes are to be avoided. Colour may be used to highlight facilities so as to assist the partially sighted. Wall and floor surfaces should be chosen so as to minimize light reflections and sound reverberations to assist the partially sighted or the hard of hearing.

5. INTERIOR RAMPS

5.1 Slopes

A slope of 1:20 is considered level, 1:15 adequate and 1:12 being the absolute maximum slope permitted for a comfortable ramp for wheelchair bound or ambulant disabled persons.

5.2 Dimensions and details

A minimum clear, unobstructed ramp width of 1 m and a surface width of 1.2 m (including kerb) are required. Kerbs or solid balustrades should be provided on the open sides of ramps. The maximum length permitted between landings depends on the slope of the ramp. This maximum length is 10 m for slopes of 1:15 to 1:20 and 5 m for slopes of 1:12 to 1:15. Top and bottom landings must be at least 1.2 m long with intermediate landings being 1.5 m long, measured clear of any door swing. A non-slip surface is required.

5.3 Handrails

A suitable continuous handrail is required on each side of a ramp if the ramp length is over 2 m. Handrails should have a maximum diameter of 45 mm to 55 mm together with a 45 mm clearance between the wall and the handrail. Ramped corridors could be equipped where required with adequate handrails on at least one side to assist those who have difficulty in walking even if the slight slope may not require it.

6. ACCESSIBLE LIFTS

As defined in Part M of the Building Regulations, an accessible lift must have a clear landing of at least 1500 mm × 1500 mm in front of the door which must provide a clear width of 800 mm. The lift car must be at least 1100 mm wide by 1400 mm deep. Landing and car controls are to be between 900 mm and 1200 mm above finished floor level. A support rail, 35 mm in diametre, 900 mm from the floor level is required inside the car. Part M also describes other requirements involving tactile indications near the lift buttons, visual and voice indications and signalling systems.

7. STAIRWAYS

Accessibility for disabled people is assured by lifts, corridors and ramps yet staircases should not be ignored since many ambulant disabled and partially sighted people will use them. Interior stairs should have a minimum tread depth of 250 mm and maximum riser height of 170 mm with landings of a minimum size of 1200 mm clear of any door swings. Handrails on each side of the stairwell should have a maximum diameter of 45 mm to 50 mm, be continuous and extend 300 mm into a landing. Handrails should be installed at a height of 900 mm above the nosing line of the steps and 1000 mm above landings. Integral stair nosings and handrails should be easily distinguishable and open risers are to be avoided. A tactile strip at the top of a stair warns of an impending change of level and each step nosing should be made easily visible by the use of strips of contrasting colour. Each riser should be uniform and not be greater than 170 mm high. Stairways should be at least 1 m wide with a maximum height of 1.2 m between landings

8. ACCESSIBLE WCS

8.1 *Minimum room size*

The absolute minimum size of a WC accessible by a wheelchair-bound person is 1500 mm × 2000 mm. A minimum size of 2000 mm by 2500 mm permits a peninsular layout of the toilet bowl (central and away from the wall). This may permit a wheelchair-bound person to transfer onto the toilet from either side but then the basin will not be usable from a seated position on the toilet which is a desirable feature. It is therefore preferable in larger accessible compartments to position the toilet as described in 8.4 as in a smaller (1500 mm × 2000 mm) WC.

8.2 *Door width and swing*

Doors of accessible WCs should provide a 800 mm clear width, however, Part M of the Building Regulations requires a 1000 mm doorset (875 mm clear opening). For safety reasons WC doors should always open outwards even though larger accessible WCs may have the required internal clear space for a wheelchair to permit the door to open inwards. An outward opening door permits easy access into the WC in case of an emergency where the wheelchair or person may be blocking an inward opening door. The door swing should be handed to provide easy access from the main approach. Outward opening doors of WCs should not block busy corridors. In such circumstances a sliding door should be considered.

8.3 *Door ironmongery*

Ironmongery should be clearly visible and be easily operable. The door should be equipped with a lever type handle on the outside and a horizontal push/pull rail on the inside. The lock should permit access from the outside in the event of an emergency.

8.4 *Toilet bowl and WC layout*

Installation of the toilet bowl at approximately 500 mm, centre line to side wall, permits easy use of vertical and horizontal wall-mounted grab bars on one side of the WC. Vertical and horizontal support rails on the wall behind the toilet bowl, as well as a hinged support rail on the other side of the toilet bowl permits the lateral transfer of a disabled person from a wheelchair onto the toilet bowl. This method of transfer also requires a clear wheelchair space adjacent to the toilet bowl, and a hinged support rail that folds vertically or swings back against the wall so as not to interfere with lateral transfer onto the toilet. The top of the toilet bowl should be from 450 mm to 475 mm above finished floor level. The clear door opening should also be in line with the clear wheelchair space that is adjacent to the toilet. If there is more than one accessible WC then the option of left or right transfer should be provided.

8.5 *Basin and related fixtures*

The basin, soap and towel/dryer facilities of accessible WCs should be usable from a seated position on the toilet. The edge of the basin should be at approximately 250 mm in front of the front edge of the toilet bowl. A single lever water mixer controlling both water temperature and flow is preferred. The hot water should be thermostatically controlled. If the water source is at least 100 mm in front of the rear of the basin and 100 mm above the edge of the basin then hand rinsing is possible from a seated position. The choice of basin needs to resolve the conflict between the need for minimal interference with transfers from a wheelchair onto the toilet bowl (basin close to wall) and generous space under the basin for clearance of legs of a wheelchair-bound person (basin sticks out from wall). The rim of the basin should be at 750 mm above finished floor level.

8.6   *Other fixtures*

A mirror at least 400 mm × 900 mm in size should be mounted at 900 mm above finished floor level. A small, low shelf is required near the basin for bags, etc. The coat hook should be fixed 1400 mm above finished floor level.

8.7   *Alarm*

A pull-cord alarm should be fitted and reach to within 150 mm above finished floor level. An alarm should be linked to a manned station (where required) and be visual as well as audible.

8.8   *Controls*

Lighting should operate via an infrared sensor or an easily accessible pull-cord that reaches within 1000 mm of finished floor level. The pull-cord should contrast with background finishes and be distinctly different from the alarm pull-cord to avoid confusion.

8.9   *Finishes and contrast*

Fittings should contrast with background floor and wall finishes. Floor finish should be non-slip and non-reflective.

8.10   WCs *for ambulant disabled persons*

Accessible WCs for ambulant disabled people are smaller in size (800 mm × 1500 mm minimum) and are equipped with a full width door opening outwards and wall mounted vertical and horizontal support rails on each side. They can thus be integrated into regular WCs since all other facilities can be shared with non-disabled persons.

9. WORK SPACES, EATING FACILITIES AND DRESSING TABLES

9.1   *Space and dimensions*

Wheelchair users need more space whether they are seated at a work station, dining table or dressing table. A desk or table width of 900 mm is preferred with a depth of 600 mm where reach is required to the back wall or controls, etc. Desk/table height should be 800 mm (maximum). A minimum space underneath of 400 mm deep by 650 mm high permits knee access with a depth of 600 mm permitting a better approach. A clear height of 760 mm permits the arms of most models of wheelchairs to pass under the counter. The reach of a wheelchair user at a dressing table depends on how far the wheelchair goes under the table as well as the depth of the work surface. This must be considered when placing electric switches and sockets and other controls.

9.2   *Seminar rooms*

The various seminar and meeting rooms should also provide facilities for people with hearing impairments as well as a variety of seating facilities for ambulant disabled persons and space for wheelchairs.

9.3   *Reception desks*

In various locations reception desks and serving counters are to be usable by wheelchair users. This involves a maximum counter height of 800 mm above the finished floor level with a minimum 400 mm deep by 650 mm high clear space under the counter. A minimum clear height of 700 mm is preferred under the counter with a clear height of 760 mm permitting the arms of a wheelchair to fit under the counter. A minimum of 1000 mm of counter length should provide this clearance. A minimum dimension of 800 mm is required between the counter top and any barriers behind allowing the wheelchair to circulate. At certain reception desks an aid to communication such as an induction loop, well signed, is desirable to assist the hard of hearing.

9.4 Telephones and vending machines

Public telephones should be installed with consideration of their use by disabled people. This involves a low installation permitting comfortable telephone use from a wheelchair seated position, a shelf, a grab rail for ambulant disabled persons and an inductive coupler enabling people with hearing aids to use them. The top button should not be at more than 1400 mm above finished floor level with the card slot at 1200 mm above finished floor level. These heights give guidance to the positioning of other fixtures such as vending machines which are to be operable from a wheelchair position.

9.5 Signage and way-finding

A well-defined system of signage and way-finding, which also assists the partially sighted is a great aid to all people. Signage involving fire safety is of particular importance.

9.6 Lighting levels and contrast

People who are visually impaired appreciate acceptable levels of lighting as well as good colour and tonal contrast on obstacles, doors, door hardware, switches and controls and in all other areas where it is beneficial to partially-sighted persons. Reflective and glossy materials should be avoided and non-slip flooring specified.

9.7 Fire safety

Part M of the Building Regulations deals with both access into, and circulation in buildings for disabled people, as well as certain facilities available for them in buildings. It excludes specific requirements for fire safety for disabled persons which are covered in BS 5588, part 8 in terms of protected entrances and exits, places of refuge, evacuation lifts, assistance to disabled people in an emergency and communication devices such as fire alarms and visual signals, etc.

NOTES

Chapter 1

1. McGough, S., *Design For Special Needs*, 47, September/December 1988.
2. Pevsner, N, *Buildings of England*, started in 1951 (2nd edition in progress).
3. Kelsall, Frank, Historic Buildings Adviser, English Heritage, from comments made during a seminar at the Centre for Accessible Environments, November 1994.
4. Goldsmith, Selwyn., The Ideology of Designing for the Disabled. *Design for Special Needs*, 31, May/August 1984, pp. 10–15.
5. Royal Commission on the Historical Monuments of England, *National Building Records, An Inventory of the Historical Monuments in the City of York*, Volume IV 1975.
6. Section 2.3 of the *Guidelines to the Burra Charter: Cultural Significance*, adopted by the Australian National Committee of the International Council on Monuments and Sites, April, 1984, revised April 1988.
7. See generally, B. M. Feilden and J. Jokilehto, *Management Guidelines for World Cultural Heritage Sites*, draft B. M. Feilden and J. Jokilehto; *The Australian ICOMOS Charter for the Conservation of Places of Cultural Significance* (the Burra Charter) and subsequent *Guidelines to the Burra Charter: Cultural Significance*. Other sources include: *The International Charter for the Conservation and Restoration of Monuments and Sites*, ICOMOS 1966.
8. From J. Jokilehto, *Evaluation and Assessment of Heritage Resources and Treatments*, a paper presented at The Institute of Advanced Architectural Studies, University of York, October 1992.
9. Ibid.
10. See generally D. Mason and V. Shacklock, *Restoration to Conservation: The Study and Treatment of Historic Buildings and Monuments in Britain, Journal of Architectural Conservation*, 1, March 1995.
11. PPG 15 replaced the earlier guidance of DoE Circular 8/87. It covers listed buildings in England and Wales. For Scotland equivalent guidance is published by the Scottish Office *Memorandum of Guidance on Listed Buildings and Conservation Areas* 1993; general guidance is contained National Planning Policy Guidance (Scotland) 1994 (NPP 65); and Planning Advice Note (PAN 42).

   For a general reference on heritage legislation for England, Wales, Northern Ireland and Scotland see P. Cooling et al., *Legislation for the Built Environment: A Concise Guide* Donhead, 1993.

   The relevant planning and conservation acts vary by region and by the type of structure.

   Listed buildings and structures within conservation areas: England and Wales: the National Heritage Act (1983); Planning (Listed Buildings and Conservation Areas) Act 1990; generally, Town and Country Planning Act 1990. Scotland, Town and Country Planning Scotland Act (1992).

   For monuments and archaeological sites: England, Wales and Scotland: Ancient Monument and Archaeological Areas Act 1979; guidance: National Planning Policy Guideline (NPPG 5) Archaeology and Planning 1994, Scottish Office: Environment Department Planning Advice Note (PAN 42) Archaeology – the Planning Process and Scheduled Monument Procedures: 1994 Scottish Office: Environment Department.

   Northern Ireland: Historic Monuments and Archaeological Objects Act (Northern Ireland) 1995.
12. PPG 15 section 1.1.

13. PPG section 3.8.
14. PPG 15 section 3.11.
15. PPG 15 section 2.18.
16. Non-conformist churches have less cultural association with a particular building or site than churches of other denominations, making demolition an option where it would not otherwise be.
17. PPG 15 section 3.28.
18. Appeal by National Westminster Bank application numbers 4930954/F and 4930955/L, opinion letter dated 1 February 1995, issued by Inspector A. J. Wood.
19. English Heritage Guidance Note, *Easy Access to Historic Properties*, October 1995 (available free from English Heritage).

Chapter 2

1. The situation in Scotland was different from England and Wales since Part T of the Building Regulations (Scotland) (the equivalent of Part M of the Building Regulations) was applied to existing buildings, while Part M expressly does not apply to alterations of existing buildings.
2. *A Brief Guide to the Disability Discrimination Act*, DL 40, November 1995, published by Disability on the Agenda, under the supervision of the Minister of Disabled People.
3. Trevor Mitchell, Historic Buildings Adviser, from *Notes on the Assessment of Disabled Access Proposals which affect Listed Buildings*, 14 June 1993.
4. For more information contact: G. J. Meijer, ICS Access, Bluelandweg, Postbus 282, 2800 AG Gouda, The Netherlands.
5. Part M, Part T, *Designing for the Disabled*, 3rd edition, S. Goldsmith, RIBA Publications, 1976; *Designing for Accessibility; an Introductory Guide*, Tessa Palfreyman and Stephen Thorpe, Centre for Accessible Environments.

Chapter 3

1. Trevor Mitchell, Historic Buildings Adviser, from *Notes on the Assessment of Disabled Access Proposals which affect Listed Buildings*, 14 June 1993.

Chapter 4

1. PPG 15 section 3.3.
2. PPG 15 section 3.3.
3. English Heritage Guidance Note, *Easy Access to Historic Properties*, October 1995.
4. *The National Trust and Disabled Visitors*, the National Trust (updated annually).

BIBLIOGRAPHY

Appleton J, *Access to Arts Buildings*. Scottish Arts Council, 1996

Barker P, Barrick and Wilson, *Building Sight*, RNIB & HMSO, 1995

Disability Scotland, *Disabled Access Guide*, 1993

Earnscliffe J, *In Through the Front Door*, Arts Council of England

Foster L, *Perspectives on Access to Museums and Galleries in Historic Buildings*. Museums and Galleries Commission, 1996

Goldsmith S, *Designing for the Disabled*, (3rd), RIBA Publications, London, 1976

Holmes-Siesdle J, *Barrier-Free Design*. Butterworth Architecture, 1996

Journal of Heritage & Environmental Interpretation, *Enabling Access Interpretation*, Feb. 1996

Museums and Galleries Commission, *Disability Resource Directory*, 1993

Palfreyman T and Thorpe S, *Designing for Accessibility An Introductory Guide*, Centre for Accessible Environments, 1993

Pearson A, *Arts For Everyone, Guidance on Provision for Disabled People* Carnegie UK and Centre for Accessible Environments, 1985

RNIB, *Discovering Museums*, HMSO

RNIB *Making Museums Accessible*, Sept. 1995

Scottish Arts Council, *National Lottery Information and Guidance Notes*.

Scottish Home and Health Department, *Fire Safety at Work*, Home Office HMSO, 1989

Thorpe S, *Good Loo Design*, Centre for Accessible Environments, 1988

Wilson R and Barker P, *Design Insights*, RNIB, 1993

INDEX